sew what!
FLEECE

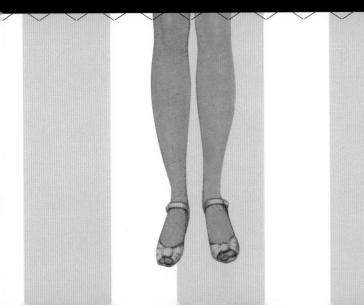

sew what! FLEECE

GET COMFY WITH 35 HEAD-TO-TOE, EASY-TO-SEW PROJECTS!

CAROL JESSOP
& CHAILA SEKORA

The mission of Storey Publishing is to serve our customers by publishing practical information that encourages personal independence in harmony with the environment.

Edited by Nancy D. Wood
Art direction by Cynthia McFarland
Cover design, interior design, and photo styling by Carol Jessop,
  Black Trout Design
Text production by Kristy L. MacWilliams

Interior Photographs by Kevin Kennefick
Illustrations by Christine Erikson

Technical writing by Anita Collins
Technical editing by Janet DuBane
Indexed by Mary McClintock

Printed in Hong Kong by Elegance
10 9 8 7 6 5 4 3 2 1

Library of Congress Cataloging-in-Publication Data

Jessop, Carol.
  Sew what! fleece / By Carol Jessop and Chaila Sekora.
    p. cm.
  Includes index.
  ISBN 978-1-58017-626-2 (hardcover w/ concealed wiro : alk. paper)
  1. Sewing. 2. Handicraft. 3. Fleece (Textile) 4. Flannel. I. Sekora, Chaila. II. Title.
TT515.J48 2007
646.4—dc22

                                                    2007016417

contents

DEAR FRIENDS,

After working on *Sew What! Skirts*, Storey's first book about sewing without a pattern, we were so inspired that we immediately starting thinking, "What's next?" Sewing with fleece seemed like the obvious choice for the next book in the series. Making clothes without a pattern was daunting at first, but fleece is so forgiving, it practically begs you to experiment. Then, Carol had her breakthrough about starting with a body template as a basis for cutting out patterns. After that, our creative freedom really took off.

We would like to thank Deborah Balmuth for launching the series and encouraging us to submit our book proposal. Thanks to your support and your belief in the concept of patternless sewing, our ideas were allowed to take root. We also want to thank our editor, Nancy Wood; without you, truly, this book would not have been possible. Thanks so much for your patience, inspiration, and knowledge.

Special appreciation goes to Anita Collins for bringing her years of technical writing experience to the party. We can come up with the designs and make them look great, but writing about how we did it fell on your shoulders. Thanks for taking on a challenging job and seeing it through.

We applaud the amazing photography team of Kevin Kennifick, Sheri Riddell, and their models for making us look so good. Thanks also to Sarah Strong, Katie Case, and Franny Shuker-Haines, our intrepid seamstresses, for testing, refining, and producing many of our designs.

Lastly, Carol thanks her mother for teaching her to sew, although her mom does not remember it.

Carol Jessop   *Chaila Sekora*

Introduction

UNLIKE YOUR EX-BOYFRIEND OR YOUR MOTHER, fleece is forgiving. It's the perfect fabric for learning to sew and design apparel, a fabric that engages both sides of your brain. Your practical left side will approve of fleece's warmth, its easy wash-and-wear maintenance, and its stain-resistant qualities. Your creative right side will love fleece's tactile feel, the vast variety of colors, prints, and textures you can choose from, and how simple it is to create with.

This is not your grandmother's sewing book. This is your permission slip to have fun, to create, and to break any or all old-school sewing rules. The *Sew What!* series is designed to free up your inner wild seamstress as you simplify your sewing and increase your enjoyment. These books are not your typical, tailored sewing construction manuals. They're more like sewing cookbooks to help you express your individuality through fabric, form, and fashion.

Each project is photographed to inspire you and is described with step-by-step instructions. You'll also see ideas and suggestions that encourage you to create your own variations. You don't have to buy a pattern to create anything you see in this book. We'll show you how to do it yourself, your way, to fit your body and your style.

So, start your love affair of sewing with fleece by designing, making, and gifting the projects found in this book. When you sew with fleece, there is no ironing, no traditional seam finishes, and no linings. Chapter 1 starts you off with easy projects that use just a single layer of fleece and simple geometric shapes. You'll progress from sewing scarves, hats, and shawls to actually designing clothes with our patternless approach. By the end of this book you'll have the confidence and know-how to create indoor, outdoor, and even pet-sized fashions. A whole new sewing world awaits you!

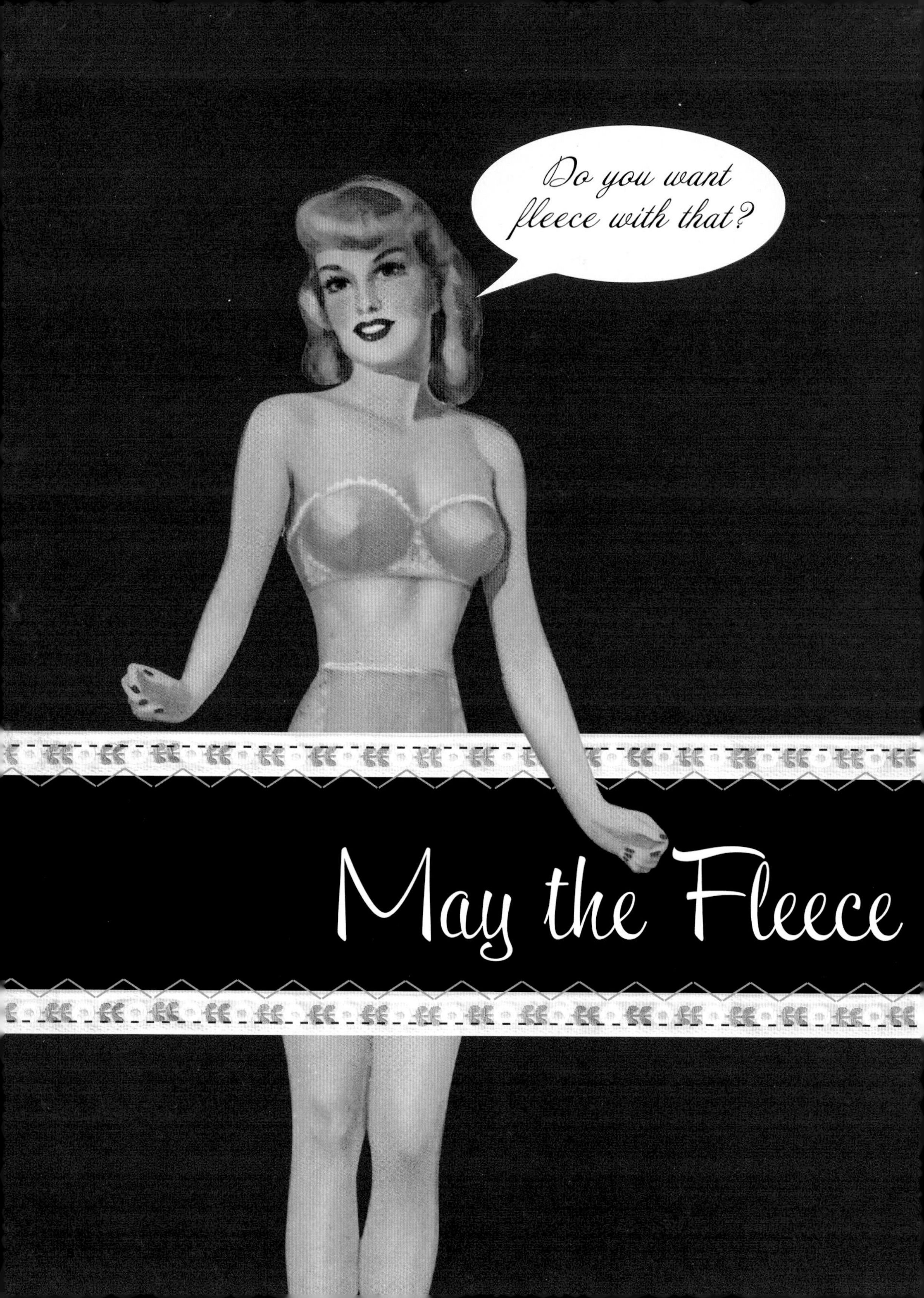

May the Fleece

$\mathcal{I}$F WE HAD TO NAME ONE UNIVERSAL FABRIC that is intuitively easy to sew, it would be fleece. This space-age fabric forever changed the way we dress for cold weather and sports. Not only is fleece comforting to wear, sewing with it is a liberating experience that naturally inspires creativity. Because fleece doesn't ravel or fray, you don't have to finish raw edges or worry about hems. You are free to make it up and do it your way!

Be with You

1

The Ultimate Fab Fabric

What is fleece anyway? This lightweight, insulating fabric is made from polyester or (believe it or not) from recycled plastic bottles! Polarfleece® was invented in 1979, in Massachusetts, by Malden Mills, and was designed to mimic wool. This man-made, high-performance fabric not only feels warm and cozy, it helps the environment, too.

Polyester fleece is a knitted fabric (constructed by interlacing loops), as opposed to a woven fabric (made on a loom). This makes fleece stretchy and unlikely to fray or ravel — like a T-shirt, which is also made of a knitted fabric. Fleece is perfect for winter wear, loungewear, sportswear, pajamas, hats, mittens, accessories, blankets, linings, and more. Kids, adults, even pets, love fleece. The following list of qualities tells us why:

- very lightweight while providing exceptional warmth
- soft against the skin
- comfortable to wear
- breathable and wicks moisture away from the body (keeps you dry)
- strong, can withstand multiple washings and dryings
- easy to care for
- fast drying
- virtually stain proof
- does not shrink or bleed color
- edges do not ravel

All of the projects in this book are made from fleece, which is one of the easiest fabrics to sew. If you are new to sewing, you probably want to start with a medium-weight fleece, leaving the high-loft and stretchy velour types for later. However, any of the projects can be made from just about any type of fleece fabric. You can start with a solid fleece and decorate it with buttons, trims, or other embellishments (such as fancy pockets); or you can select a distinctive fleece print to make your fashion statement without a lot of extra add-ons.

When buying your fabric, be sure to read the end of the *bolt* (the cardboard that the fabric is wrapped around). There, you will find information about the fabric: what it is made of, how wide it is, and how much it costs per yard. Make a note of the washing instructions for future reference.

Even though fleece does not shrink, it's still wise to prepare the fabric according to the washing instructions. When you see how your fleece reacts to being washed and dried, this may help you decide which side of the fabric you prefer to be the *right side* (the side that will be facing out when the finished clothing is worn). Always preshrink cottons and other fabrics you'll be combining with fleece by washing and drying them before you cut anything out. Although it might be tempting to skip this preparation stage, don't! You will be making your project to fit, and you surely don't want any surprises the first time you wash it.

How Much to Buy

The amount of fabric you need depends on you and what you want to make. Although we make recommendations for each project, your design choices can change what you need. How long do you want the item to be? How tall are you? How much fullness do you want?

Most polyester fleece fabrics are 54" to 65" wide, but some fabrics are as much as 68" or 72" wide. Since the average non-fleece fabric is usually 45" wide, you can typically cut a lot more pieces from a yard of fleece than from a yard of cotton. The best part is all those leftover scraps, perfect for quickie projects like hats and mittens.

We will show you the most likely layout for each project in the most common width, but when in doubt, look in a pattern book for a garment that is similar to the one you want to make, and see how much fabric the pattern recommends for your size.

FLEECE FACTS

Fleece is available in three common weights:

- Lightweight fleece (including microfleece): thin, tightly knit fabric with a soft hand (drapability)
- Medium-weight fleece: moderate weight and warmth, usually double-faced (fuzzy on both sides)
- Heavyweight fleece: heaviest fleece for use in extremely cold temperatures

You'll also see fleece referred to by numbers, such as 100, 200, and 300. These numbers describe the fleece's fabric weight in grams. Just remember that a higher number means that the fleece will be thicker and warmer.

curly

curly

sherpa

microfleece

microfleece

plush

sherpa

A World of Choice

Each passing year brings more varieties of fleece. With so many options, your biggest challenge may be deciding which one to try first! Here are a few types of fleece that are widely available:

- *Berber.* A curly, nubby texture on the right side with a smooth knitted wrong side.
- *Brushed.* The most common fleece, looks like a dense felted fabric.
- *Curly.* A high-loft fleece with a long silky pile on one side and a furry texture on the other.
- *Heather.* Recycled fleece with a mottled color.
- *Microfleece.* A very thin, lightweight fleece fabric that feels like chamois cloth or suede.
- *Plush.* A high-loft fleece with a velvety feel and appearance created by shearing the fabric's surface.
- *Sherpa* or *Shearling.* A bumpy texture on the right side looks like real lamb's wool; the wrong side has a smooth knitted surface.
- *Velour.* An upscale version of brushed fleece, usually more sheared and plush than regular brushed fleece.
- *Waffle.* A fleece with a gridded or waffle texture.

Fleece TLC

Since fleece is a synthetic knit fabric, it's easy to wash, wear and care for. To keep fleece looking new, keep these care pointers in mind:

- Machine-wash fleece in cool to moderately warm water using liquid detergent.
- Turn fleece clothing inside out (to prevent pilling) and wash with like garments.
- Machine-dry using a low setting.
- Don't overdry fleece in the dryer.
- Don't use dryer sheets and fabric softeners, which may reduce water-repellant features.

- Don't use a hot iron, which will melt fleece. "Finger-press" your fleece instead.

- Don't wash fleece with rough-surfaced items such as jeans; this will abrade and pill the surface.

- Avoid washing fleece with items that produce lint such as towels. Fleece picks up lint.

After caring for your fleece fabric, take care of your sewing equipment, too. You'll be surprised by how much lint is created when cutting and sewing with fleece. Take time to wipe your scissors clean. Use a lint brush to clean under your sewing machine's throat plate and check moving parts that need oiling. You may need to do this often during your projects, not just at the end.

Adaptable Fleece

The projects in this book are designed to work well with fleece, but you still have some decisions to make. Choose the best quality fleece fabric you can afford so that the garments and projects you create will last and look great over time. Some fleece fabrics will *pill*, which means they abrade and get little balls on the surface like a worn-out sweater. The best fleeces are designed with anti-pill features. You can also find anti-odor, water-resistant, and wind-resistant varieties.

If and when you start branching off into other patterns outside the scope of this book, be sure to choose projects that will complement fleece's qualities. Since fleece can be a bulky fabric, avoid patterns with multiple seams that need to lie flat. Also, since fleece will melt if pressed with a hot iron, don't choose patterns that require pressing to shape the garment. Once you've gained some experience working with fleece, you can sometimes adapt patterns by omitting the linings and facings. If you make one of the jackets in chapter 4, you'll see that it's possible to create collars and entire garments from a single layer of fleece.

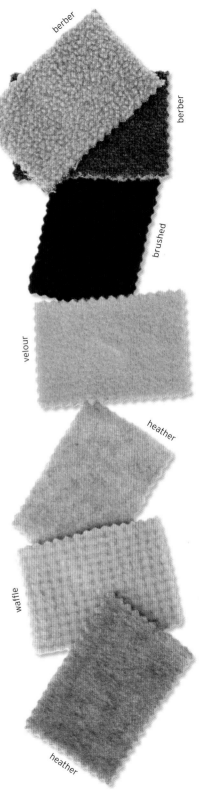

berber

berber

brushed

velour

heather

waffle

heather

Selvage

Crosswise grain
(greatest stretch)

grainline

This symbol indicates the crosswise grain, or direction of greatest stretch. Watch for it on the cutting diagrams for the projects.

Good to Know

Following are some important concepts to know about fabric in general and fleece in particular. Learning the terminology makes it easier to understand instructions and sort out which end is up when it's time to cut out your project.

- The **selvage** (or selvedge) is the long finished edge on either side of the fleece — not the edge that is cut when the fabric is measured, cut, and sold by the yard. The selvage is usually a bit thicker and sturdier than the rest of the fleece, and varies in appearance depending on the machinery used to make the fabric. Depending on the fleece and the project, you may want to trim off or avoid the selvage when you cut out your fabric pieces.

- The **grainline** of a fabric refers to threads running parallel to (in the same direction as) the selvage. Sometimes this is called the *straight* (grain) of the fabric. The *crosswise grain* runs from selvage to selvage and has more "give" or stretch. Fleece can have significant stretch along its crosswise grain, and some have a lot of stretch in both directions. Test your fabric by stretching it along the grainlines.

- The **weight** is the density of the fleece, which affects its drapability or *hand*. Medium-weight fleeces are fuzzy on both sides and are suitable for most projects. Heavyweight fleeces are thick and dense which makes them best for outwear garments. Microweight fleeces have a soft hand and can be used for both accessories and garments.

- Another thing to notice is **nap**, which indicates which end of the fabric goes "up." If the fleece has a one-way or *directional* design, the nap is fairly obvious — if there are horses in the design, you want them to be upright when you put on the finished garment. On most smooth fabrics without a design, you will not be able to see nap. If you run your hand in one direction, the nap is smooth; if you run your hand the opposite way, it feels rough. You will want to cut all your pattern pieces with the nap going in the same direction.

Right or Wrong

Usually, both sides of fleece fabric look great, and it might be difficult to see much of a difference between the two. However, there usually is one side that was intended to be the right side, especially if the fleece has a water-repellent finish. For most fleece fabrics, there's a way to quickly tell which is the right side. With both hands, tug on the fabric along the lengthwise grain (parallel to the selvage); the fabric will curl to the right side. Try tugging on the crosswise grain (perpendicular to the selvage); the fabric will curl to the wrong side.

Here are some other ways to tell the difference. The right side of fleece will usually:

- Have printed words along the selvage.
- Look more plush and brushed than the wrong side.
- Look very crisp and clear (if a printed-design fabric).
- Repel water better (if a water-repellant fabric).
- Not pill (after prewashing).
- Feel softer than the wrong side.

Ultimately, with fleece it's hard to go wrong. Simply decide which side looks best to you. After you choose a right side, be consistent throughout the project. It's a good idea to mark your fabric pieces with chalk or removable tape so it's easy to tell at a glance which side you need to work with.

THICK AND THIN

When using a heavyweight or thick fleece, cut the pattern pieces through a single layer at a time. This not only avoids a tendency for the second layer to shift, it's easier than cutting through two layers of dense fabric.

pssst...

CHECK THE STRETCH

The direction of the crosswise grain, or stretch, is more important than you may think. Picture a pair of mittens, for instance. If you've made them to fit perfectly, they need to be able to stretch at the wrist when you put them on, otherwise you can't get them over the width of your hand. If you made them with the stretch going the wrong way, you may have to toss them out and start over. So, always check the direction of the stretch *before* you cut.

Generally, you'll cut out garments with the crosswise grain stretching horizontally around your body, hand, or head, rather than along the length.

GETTiNG FANCY

You can probably make all of the projects in this book with the standard presser feet that come with your machine. However, if you select fleece that is very thick or slippery, you might want to invest in an even-feed foot, commonly used by quilters to keep two layers of fabric from slipping around while being stitched. Other options are a roller foot or a Teflon foot.

Before You Start

We assume that you have a basic sewing machine and can find the instruction booklet that came with it. (Replacement manuals can often be found online.) You don't need anything brand new or fancy, just the basics — although you will need a zigzag option for fleece. If you have never sewn a stitch on your machine before, or if you've forgotten everything you thought you knew, read your manual. It will be your guide for specific ways to use your machine, such as how to make buttonholes. Once you can thread your machine and fill the bobbin, get out some scrap fleece and practice some stitching. Try out the zigzag setting, and adjust the machine tension as needed. Take your time, experiment, and have some fun.

Your machine probably came with several different presser feet. You will need one for straight stitching and one for zigzag stitching. Sometimes these are two separate feet; sometimes one works for both stitches. If you decide to put in zippers, you will need a zipper foot. You might also have a buttonhole attachment. Get familiar with how all of these things work.

MAKiNG TASSELS

Cut several ¼" to ½" wide strips of fleece in the direction of the greatest stretch. Pull the ends apart as far as they will go, then release one end. The fleece will automatically curl. If the strip breaks when you pull on it, cut another strip that is a little wider. Tack strips together to make a tassel.

In Your Sewing Basket

In addition to a sewing machine, you will want to have the following items on hand:

- a good pair of sharp shears used only for cutting fabric
- a pair of pinking shears (which make a zigzag edge) for decorative edging
- a small pair of scissors for clipping and trimming
- a rotary cutter and mat for cutting long straight lines
- straight pins (glass-head pins are a good choice)
- a tape measure, a wide transparent sewing ruler, and a yardstick
- a variety pack of hand-sewing needles
- a variety pack of sewing-machine needles
- a seam ripper
- a seam gauge (if you want to make hems)
- disappearing or chalk fabric markers
- fabric basting tape

rotary cutter

pinking shears

spring action scissors

PiNS AND NEEDLES

Long straight pins with big heads and very slender shafts are the best for most fleece fabrics — they're easier to see against fleece's dense pile. When stitching on fleece, you'll find that your sewing machine needles will get dull after only a few hours of sewing. Check your needle regularly for burrs and dull points, and always have spares available.

SHEAR NONSENSE

Technically, you call them scissors when the length is 6" or less and the finger holes are the same size. Shears are usually 7" to 12" long, with one larger finger hole (to fit two or more fingers). To keep fabric shears sharp, do not use them to cut paper, cardboard, or aluminum foil. After cutting into fleece fabrics, be sure to wipe the blades often with a clean piece of fabric to remove the buildup of fleece lint left behind.

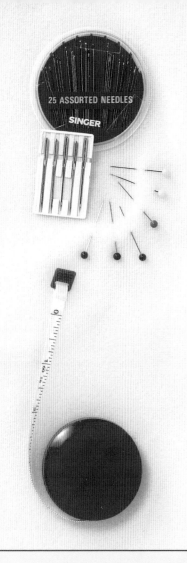

Nifty Notions

Notions refers to needles, buttons, threads, and other items associated with sewing. Read on for information about some essential notions and tools you'll want in your sewing basket.

Threads

Once you've selected fabric for a project, pick up some thread, too. The best all-purpose thread is a polyester thread, good for both hand sewing and machine sewing on almost all fabrics. Like fleece, it has some stretch.

Traditionally, thread is closely matched to the color of the fabric, so the stitches won't show. Of course, these days, anything goes. You might deliberately choose a contrasting thread to show off a nice zigzag stitch. But if you'd rather not see the stitch lines, match the thread by holding it next to the fabric (or a swatch of it) that you plan to use — it's nearly impossible to match color by memory. If you can't find exactly the right color, go with a slightly darker shade.

Needles

What's the best needle to use when machine stitching fleece? As a general rule, ballpoint or stretch needles are best for knitted fabrics like fleece, although a universal needle should work for both woven and knitted fabrics. The most important thing to remember is to choose a needle size based on the weight and density of your fabric and to change needles frequently. If you discover skipped stitches or your sewing machine isn't stitching right, you either need to switch to a larger-sized needle, or you need to replace your needle because it has become dull. Since fleece is a synthetic fabric made from dense polyester, it tends to dull needles more quickly than natural fabrics. You can also consider the newer Microtex needles which are designed to sew on dense, synthetic fabrics (like microfibers); they feature a slim point with an extrathin shaft.

RECOMMENDED SEWING MACHINE NEEDLE SiZES

Lightweight fleece: 70/10 or 75/11

Medium-weight fleece: 80/12 or 90/14

Heavyweight fleece: 100/16

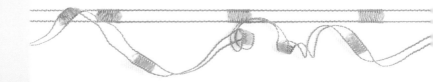

Pins

Since fleece has a fuzzy surface and often has a deep pile, pins can seem to disappear in it. To keep better track and avoid pricking your fingers on pins you can't see, use long glass-head pins. In addition, it's best to pin perpendicular to a seam instead of parallel to it. When positioning zippers and trims in place onto fleece, a quick and accurate alternative to pinning is to use basting tape. You can sew right through this thin, double-sided tape, and it dissolves the first time you wash the garment.

Rotary Cutter

To speed up your fabric prep time and reduce some of the lint that can collect on your cutting table, try cutting fleece with a 45mm or 60mm rotary cutter instead of shears. This should be done on a cutting mat designed for this purpose. The measured grid on this kind of mat can also be helpful when cutting a long straight line, such as when making a scarf. For a flawless straight line, also use a transparent ruler to press down the fleece, aligning the grid on the ruler with the grid on the mat. (*See photo, right.*)

Other Useful Items

Fleece can produce lots of lint. You'll find it handy to have canned air and a lint brush in your sewing room to help keep you, your fleece, and your sewing area tidy. Use a brush or mini-vacuum to clean the bobbin area of your sewing machine. Canned air can blow out lint from an area very quickly and easily.

Fleece has a tendency to become charged with static electricity, which makes it cling to itself as well as attract lint, dust, and animal hairs. This can be remedied with a can of anti-static spray.

If you've never used a rotary cutter, you're in for a treat. Used with a mat and transparent ruler, cutters are great for clean straight edges.

Let me slip into something more comfortable.

Tangled Up

Y OU NEED ONLY A FEW BASIC SKILLS to sew the fleece projects in this book. Some techniques might seem intimidating at first, but only because they are unfamiliar. Once you've tried them a time or two, you'll gain confidence. If you already know the basics, jump on ahead and find a fleece project you want to make. Refer back to this chapter as needed if you're not sure about some of the techniques.

in Fleece 2

It's a Stitch

WITH SO MANY DIFFERENT SEWING MACHINES out there, we can't give instructions that would apply to them all. Your sewing-machine manual and an experienced friend or family member can get you started. The rest is mostly practice. Be sure to read the section in your manual on stitch length (literally, how long the stitches are) and tension (how tightly the stitches are pulled).

Most machines have the same basic settings, which can be changed by turning a stitch-length dial. The three basic kinds of stitches you will use are:

- **normal** stitch: usually short stitches that hold a seam together

- **basting** stitch: the longest stitches on your sewing machine; these are considered temporary and easy to remove

- **zigzag** stitch: used to stitch seams, finish raw edges and for decoration. (Your machine manual will show you how to control not only how many zigzag stitches per inch, but also the width of the stitch. You may need a separate zigzag presser foot when using this stitch.)

normal stitch

narrow zigzag

wide zigzag

When sewing a woven fabric — cotton, for instance — the normal stitch setting is 10–12 stitches per inch (2 mm–2.5 mm on metric machines) and a basting stitch is 6–8 stitches per inch (3mm–4mm). However, fleece and other knitted fabrics sewn with a normal stitch setting might develop waves due to the natural stretch of the fabric. For flat seams, try one or more of the following approaches:

- Increase the stitch length to 7–9 stitches per inch (3mm–3.5mm), which is closer to a basting stitch for woven fabric. When basting fleece, make the stitch even longer.

- Change from a straight stitch to a medium-width/medium-length zigzag stitch. This is helpful when stitching areas that require a lot of stretch.

- Change the type or size of your sewing-machine needle — or sometimes the needle you're using has become dull, and it's enough just to replace it.

- Reduce the pressure of your sewing machine's presser foot.

- Change your sewing machine's presser foot. Try a using a roller foot or an even-feed foot on your machine.

The following terms are not stitch settings on a dial; they describe how stitching is used for a particular purpose:

- A **staystitch** is a line of stitches sewn in the seam allowance almost on the seamline, which prevents the seam from coming undone.

- **Topstitching** means that the stitching shows on the "top" or the right side of the fabric. This stitch is usually decorative and sewn in one or more straight parallel lines.

- **Backtack** stitches are used mostly at the beginning and end of a line of stitching to prevent it from coming undone. You don't backtack on basting stitches, as they will be pulled out later.

- **Edgestitch** means just what it sounds like: machine stitching close to the edge of a fabric piece, on the top of the right side, as when stitching a pocket on a project.

pssst...

THE MAGIC NUMBERS

It's a good idea to test your stitch length and tension when starting a new project. Sew together two scraps of the fabric you'll be using. Check (and adjust as needed) the top thread and the bobbin thread of the stitching to make sure the tension and stitch length work for that fabric and thread.

When the stitches are neither too tight nor too loose, pin a piece of paper to the scrap that identifies the stitch length, tension, and kind of thread you used. This helps if you are making more than one project at a time or have to leave the project and come back to it later.

right side

seam

wrong side
of fabric

backtack

½" seam
allowance

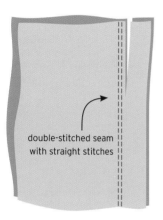

double-stitched seam
with straight stitches

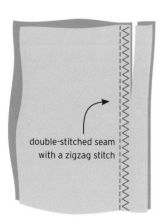

double-stitched seam
with a zigzag stitch

As It Seams

You probably know that a seam is where you sew two pieces of fabric together. The seam allowance is the leftover fabric between the stitching line and the edge of the fabric. Most commercial patterns use a ⅝" seam allowance, and quilters sew with a ¼" seam allowance. We use a ½" seam allowance, mostly because it's easier to do the math! To keep your seam stitching straight, use the guide on the plate of your machine, or put a piece of tape on the plate with the inside edge ½" from the needle hole. *(See box on page 25.)*

When sewing a seam, you usually put two pieces of fabric together, with the right sides facing each other. Line up the sides and hem edges before you sew. Most seams are backtacked at the beginning and end of the seam, except for basted seams.

A standard practice after sewing a seam is to press the seam allowances open. Why? To make the fabric lie smooth and flat — but you can't iron fleece, it's heat sensitive! So just use your fingers to smooth and press the seam open. That's called finger pressing.

If you're sewing with fleece and you find that the seam allowances curl (this can happen on a very soft knit fabric), try using a double-stitched seam. After stitching your seam, stitch a second row of stitching (either straight or zigzag) close to the first row and trim away the seam allowance close to the second row.

HEADS UP!

For the projects in this book, assume a ½" seam allowance, with right sides of the fabric together, unless the directions call for something different.

Decorative Seams

Once you've made a seam, you can move on to the next step — or, you can opt for a more personal touch. Seam allowances can be finger-pressed open or with both allowances to one side, then topstitched into place. You can use a zigzag or straight stitch, with a matching color thread or a contrasting color. Our examples show contrasting colors, mostly so you can see the seams. But one of the nicest things about making your own clothes is that you can do it your way — and no one else will be wearing anything like it!

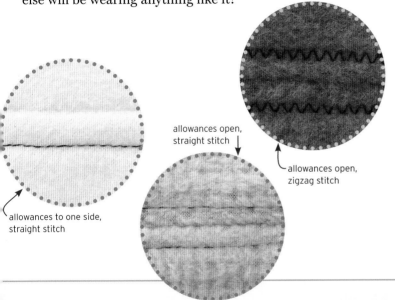

allowances open,
straight stitch

allowances open,
zigzag stitch

allowances to one side,
straight stitch

NiCE AND SMOOTH

Once you've washed your fabric, notice which is the right side (outside) of the fabric and which is the wrong side (inside). With right sides together, fold the fabric lengthwise and lay it on a cutting surface. Keep the selvages together and adjust them until there are no bubbles on the folded edge. You may want to pin the selvages together in a few places to keep the fabric edges from sliding around.

LiNE iT UP!

Most sewing machines have marks to the right of the presser foot to help you measure and align your seams. The longest line is usually at $5/8$", the seam width most commonly used. Since we use $1/2$" as our standard, place a strip of tape $1/2$" from your presser foot to keep your seams uniform and straight. (*See right*: We used blue masking tape.) As you move the fabric under the needle, line up the edge of the fabric with the tape.

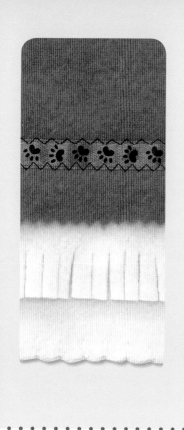

The Cutting Edge

There are so many shortcuts to sewing with fleece. Because fleece won't ravel when you cut it, you'll save time by not having to finish seam edges. If you so choose, you don't even have to make hems. Here are some ideas for how to handle fleece's cut edges:

- Decorative cut edges using pinking shears, decorative edge scissors, or decorative edge rotary blades.

- Fringe cut by hand with shears or a rotary cutter.

- Hand-stitching with embroidery or crochet thread, for instance a blanket stitch.

- Serged edge using a serger or overlock machine.

- Decorative edge using machine embroidery stitches.

Non-Fleece Raw Edges

Some of the projects in this book combine traditional woven fabrics with fleece. Non-fleece fabrics may require some attention to raw edges. For instance, on both sides of any seam is a seam allowance — and two raw edges of fabric. These edges will not show, because they're on the inside of the garment. However, depending on the fabric, these edges could fray or ravel. You'll see for yourself when you prewash the fabric. Some woven fabrics fray very little, and you don't have to finish the edges. Some raveled edges can be a real mess, bunching up and making your seamlines look bumpy.

Whether or how you finish those raw edges is entirely up to you. Everyone who sews has a favorite finish. Most purchased garments have serged finishing, which requires a special machine. However, there are plenty of simple alternatives:

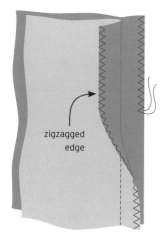

zigzagged edge

- **Zigzag Stitch.** Using the zigzag stitch, sew every raw edge of each seam with the outside point of the stitch at the edge of the fabric.

- **Turned Edge.** This is just what it sounds like — you turn over the edge and stitch it down. For a neat, accurate line, start by sewing a single line of stitching about ¼″ from the raw edge. Use this as a guide to fold the edge (toward the body of the garment); press, then sew another line of stitching close to the fold. As you gain more practice, you will be able to press without a guide — or even skip the pressing altogether and just fold the edge under as you sew.

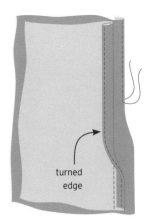

turned
edge

- **Pinking.** Pinking is very easy and it is well worth investing in good quality pinking shears. First, sew a straight line of stitching ¼" from the edge. Use pinking shears to cut off the outer edge as shown.

- **Fray Preventer.** There are several fray-prevention glues on the market; just follow the directions on the bottle. Be careful with the glue, or you might end up with glue where you don't want it. Place a piece of heavyweight paper between the seam allowance and the fabric to catch any stray drips.

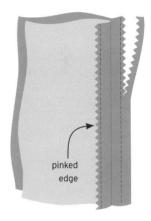

pinked
edge

Sewing a Curved Line

The majority of seams in this book are straight seams — a piece of cake. One exception is the mittens, which have inward (concave) and outward (convex) curves. Whenever you sew a curved edge it helps to clip or notch the seam allowance of the curved piece before turning the right sides out. Otherwise, the seam will pull or bunch up when you turn it. Generally notches are cut into outward curves, and inward curves are clipped. The idea is to cut up to — but not through — the seam stitching. How many clips or notches you need, and how far apart to cut them, is for you to decide. Do whatever works for the shape you are sewing.

In woven fabrics, even milder curves like those in a waistband, crotch, or armhole need clipping. Stretchy fleece, however, can usually accommodate such curves — yet one more shortcut advantage to using this fabric!

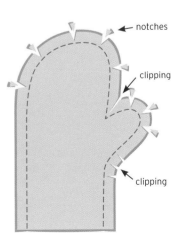

notches

clipping

clipping

The Bottom Line

A non-fleece garment usually has a hem along the bottom and the ends of sleeves or leg to finish off edges that would otherwise fray. While you don't need to hem fleece, you might decide to add one for a more finished look or to add more weight to an edge.

Folded Hem

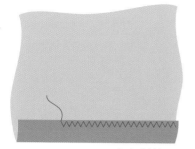

single-fold hem
with zigzag

The width of your hem depends on the project. The hem we use most often in this book is the ½" singlefold hem. However, when you make something like a jacket or robe that might need more weight at the hemline, 1" to 2" works better, or even try a double-fold hem.

1. Fold the bottom edge of the garment to the inside by ½" (or your chosen width) and pin it. For a consistent hem, a seam gauge comes in handy — measure at several points along the hem as you pin. (For a double-fold hem, simply fold twice as you measure and pin.)

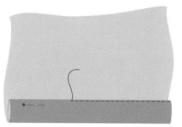

double-fold hem
with straight stitich

2. Stitch as close to the top fold as you can with a straight or zigzag stitch. Some presser feet are designed to keep your stitches straight when sewing very close to an edge. The bobbin stitches will show on the outside of the garment, so choose your thread color accordingly.

Fringed Hem

fringed hem

A fringed hem works well on any fleece. Decide how long you want the fringe to be, for example: 2". Make a guideline by stitching a straight or zigzag stitch 2" from the edge all around the hem. Or, you can use chalk to measure and mark a line 2" from the edge on the wrong side of the fabric.

To make the fringe, cut the fleece into ⅜", ½" (or wider) strips up to the stitch line or chalk line. The fringe can be cut straight up and down, diagonally, or otherwise. Since fleece won't fray, you can be as creative as you please.

Button It

A jacket or robe can be nicely finished off with a button and buttonhole. You'll need to plan ahead, though. Your sewing machine might have a special buttonhole feature (check your manual), but if it doesn't, all you need is a zigzag stitch. There should be directions for that with your machine, too, so we won't go into the details. However, here are a few pointers:

- Test sew a buttonhole on scrap fleece fabric before stitching your project. Since fleece stretches, it's best to use a stabilizer underneath your fabric, such as a second layer of fleece, a nonfusible nonwoven interfacing, or a tear-away stabilizer product. In a pinch, you could even use a lightweight tracing paper — just line it up behind the fabric and stitch through both, then tear or cut away any excess paper when you're done.

- To prevent the fabric from waving, adjust your machine's stitch length to an open zigzag stitch instead of the dense satin stitch usually used for buttonholes.

- Place the buttonhole on the right-hand side of a jacket opening. Sew the button on the left-hand side of the jacket opening.

- The buttonhole should be horizontal, which keeps the button from popping out of the hole as you move around.

- Use a disappearing fabric marker and a ruler to draw where you want the buttonhole to be. Make the horizontal line the exact width of the button you want to use.

- When stitching the buttonhole, leave a narrow gap between the upper and lower horizontal rows of stitching. Then use a sharp seam ripper to slit the gap open. Take care not to cut the long vertical stitches on either end.

FLEECE CLOSURE OPTIONS

- Buttons and buttonholes
- Zippers
- Snaps
- Grommets
- Velcro
- Ties, ribbons, cording
- Hooks, clasps, toggles
- Frog closures

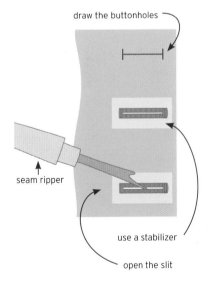

draw the buttonholes

seam ripper

use a stabilizer

open the slit

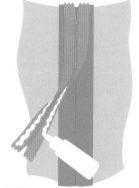

Zip It

Putting in a zipper doesn't have to be hard. Really. Like anything else, it just takes practice. While you're learning, it's best to stay away from invisible zippers and stick to the basic steps for a centered zipper. (Instructions for a centered or lapped treatment usually come with the zipper; if not, there are numerous helpful instructions online.) Here are few pointers:

1. Baste the portion of the seam where the zipper will be.

2. Apply fabric glue or basting tape to the right side of the zipper, on either side of the zipper teeth. With the zipper closed, position the top of the zipper head on the wrong side at the top of the seamline, *not* at the top of the fabric. Lay the zipper teeth directly over the basted seamline. If you prefer, pin the zipper in place and baste, removing the pins as you stitch.

STEP 2

3. Turn the garment over and lay it flat, right side up. Center a strip of ½"-wide clear tape (the same length as the zipper) over the seam. This will be your stitching guide, so make sure the tape reaches just below the bottom zipper stop. *Note:* Test the tape first on a scrap of your fabric. If tape is not an option, use chalk and a ruler to make ¼" stitching lines on either side of the zipper.

After sewing the zipper in place, use a seam ripper to carefully remove the basting stitches in the seam in front of the zipper. You may need a little something extra to secure the top of the zipper opening. The simplest solution is a hook and eye. The holes on either side of each part are for hand-sewing them to your garment.

STEP 3

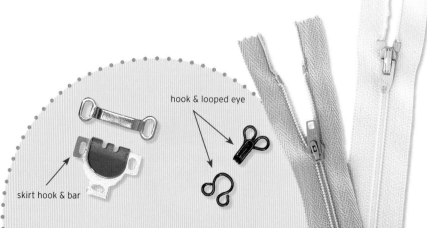

hook & looped eye

skirt hook & bar

FINISHED ZIPPER

Embellishments

Now for the real secret to making a unique garment of your very own design — embellishments! There is no end to what you might try! Trims are available by the truckload in nearly every fabric store. These include rickracks, laces, ribbons, braids, and beading. Be bold and try something different! Some trims are finished on both edges, and some only on one edge. Finished trims such as rickrack can be topstitched directly onto the fabric. One-edged trims should be sewn with the unfinished edge underneath the fabric edge or into a seam.

Who Needs a Pattern?

The trouble with commercial patterns is that they are made for a generic person, not for your unique body. You may end up making so many adjustments to a pattern that it's a waste of time and money. In this book, we show you how to measure and plan your projects and accessories by drawing directly on the fabric or by making your own unique paper pattern that can be used again and again.

How loosely or tightly you like your garments to fit is also up to you. Generally you want to add *ease* (a little extra room) so things don't feel skintight. Try adding 2"–4" to your bust, waist, or hip measurements, in addition to each ½" seam allowance.

After you have made your first jacket or skirt, and before you put in the zipper or elastic, try it on. If it is bigger than you like, take in the side seams. If it is smaller than you like, change the seam allowance. Mark changes on your paper pattern, so it will be just the way you like it next time. When you find what works for you and your body type, stick with it.

FLEECE TIP

Always place your pins perpendicular to the seam so you can see them easily in the fleece's pile.

EASIER MATH

When figuring out pattern dimensions, sometimes you need to divide a number that includes a fraction. Refer to the conversions below to do your math on a calculator.

⅛ = 0.125

¼ = 0.25

⅜ = 0.375

½ = 0.5

⅝ = 0.625

¾ = 0.75

⅞ = 0.875

METRIC CONVERSIONS

For those of you using metric measurements, here are some basic conversion formulas:

Multiply inches x 2.54 to get centimeters

Multiply feet x .305 to get meters

Multiply yards x .9144 to get meters

FOR A HEALTHY DOSE OF INSTANT GRATIFICATION, try some of the quick and easy fleece projects in this chapter. What an inspiration — to stay warm and look great at the same time! You'll want to make these winners again and again for yourself, friends, and family.

Give Fleece a Chance

Warm up with some cozy fleece projects!

WHERE DO YOU BEGIN WHEN SEWING PROJECTS WITH FLEECE? It makes sense to start small, with accessories and gifts. Not only is it good practice, it's fun! The projects in this chapter can be made with minimal effort. In no time you'll be creating fabulous items to wear or give away. You'll find inspiring ideas for making scarves, shawls, hats, mittens, and all kinds of warmers for your neck, hands, legs, and ears.

The best part about fleece is that you can make many projects with just a one layer of material. Since fleece doesn't ravel or fray, you don't need to finish the seams. There's more room to be creative! You can start with the *Pretty in Pink* scarf or the *Wrap It Up* shawl, each made from a single layer of fabric. These two don't have any major seams, just a few lines of stitching where the decorations are attached. What could be easier?

Once you get the feel of sewing with fleece, the sky's the limit. There are endless possibilities for creating great accessories in your choice of color, texture, and style. You'll see how easily fleece combines with ribbons, trims, appliqués, beads, lace, buttons, tassels, and more. Whatever look you prefer, you can create it in fleece — classic or sophisticated, rugged or tailored, sporty or fun.

Buttons, Trims, and Fringe, oh my!

Here are some winning combinations
to get your ideas cooking.

Pretty in Pink

When you're looking for a fast and easy elegant gift, this fleece scarf is the one to make. It's frilly, cozy, and chic! Our scarf has a wide, sheer organza ribbon framed by two narrow velvet ribbons. But the design possibilities are endless, with your choice of ribbons, trims, or appliqués. Make one for each of your girl friends in colors and styles to match each personality.

Stuff You Need

¼ yard of 58"-60" medium-weight fleece

1 yard of ⅝" velvet ribbon

½ yard of 1½" organza ribbon

Matching or contrasting polyester thread

What You'll Do

Cut out the scarf

Embellish it

Make the fringe

Our finished size: 8" x 60"

MAKE IT!

1. *Cut it out.* The only tricky part about this project is making straight cuts along the sides. This is where a rotary cutter and mat come in. (*See page* 19.) On a cutting mat, lay the fabric out flat and cut an 8" x 60" rectangle (or desired size). Or, fold the fabric in half and cut a rectangle that is 8" x 30". If you cut the fleece folded, check the edges along the fold when you open up the scarf. If your cut was not straight, you may have a bump or an indentation. Trim as needed. ***Note:*** If your scarf is wider than 8", you'll need more ribbon than what is listed.

2. *Embellish with ribbons.* To copy our scarf, cut the organza ribbon into two 9" pieces. Pin or baste the ribbons across the right side of the scarf, about 2½" away from each end. Trim the raw edges of the ribbon even with the scarf edges. Cut the velvet ribbon into four 9" pieces and pin it to the scarf on either side of the organza, overlapping it by about ⅛". Turn under the raw ends of the velvet ribbon to match the width of the scarf. Stitch through all layers along both sides of each velvet ribbon, backtacking at the ends.

3. *Create the fringe.* Cut the fleece at the ends of the scarf into narrow strips approximately 1½" long and ½" wide, stopping about ½" away from the velvet ribbon. (*See page* 28.)

60"

8"   STEP 1

STEP 2

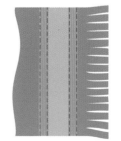

STEP 3

TO FRAY OR NOT TO FRAY

Ribbons that are cut to the width of the scarf and stitched in place might fray during washing and handling. If you like the frayed look, no problem. Otherwise, turn under the ribbon ends and stitch them in place. As an alternative, apply a non-fray product or clear nail polish to the ends of the ribbon.

Wrap It Up

Drape this shawl over an evening dress and you are ready for a night on the town. You'll feel pampered, cozy, and elegant. A strategically placed mini-pocket is just the right size for a bit of cash, a credit card, or lipstick. Or make a more casual version — perfect for snuggling up at the movies.

Stuff You Need

2 yards of 58"-60" microfleece or 1 yard of 68"-100" microfleece

1¾ yard (or more) of 2½" beaded ribbon fringe

1 button, ⅝" diameter

Matching or contrasting polyester thread

What You'll Do

Cut out a rectangle

Embellish with trim

Stitch the pocket

Make a buttonhole

Stitch the pocket flap

Sew on a button

Our finished size: 27" x 72"

MAKE IT!

1. *Cut it out.* Ultimately, the length and width of the shawl is up to you. If your fabric is 58"-60" wide and you want a shawl longer than 60", buy two yards and cut parallel to the selvage (the shawl will be 72" long; see diagram). For fleece that is 68"-100" wide, cut from selvage to selvage from less than a yard of fabric. Either way, use a rotary cutter, straight edge, and cutting mat (*see page* 19) to cut a rectangle that is 27" wide and the length you prefer. Also cut two 3" x 4" rectangles for the pocket and flap. Note: For a shawl wider than 27", you'll need more beaded fringe than what is listed.

2. *Embellish.* Cut the beaded fringe into two pieces and pin it in place along the lower edges of the shawl. Turn under both ends of the trim before stitching it.

3. *Make the pocket.* Decide where you want the pocket to be, then pin one pocket piece to the right side of the fabric. Edgestitch around the pocket as shown, leaving the top edge open. Cut the shape of the pocket flap and mark where you want the buttonhole. Reinforce the buttonhole on the wrong side with non-fusible interfacing or a scrap piece of fleece. (*See page* 29.) Stitch the flap in place above the pocket and hand-sew the button onto the pocket front.

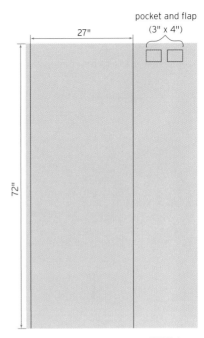

pocket and flap
(3" x 4")

27"

72"

STEP 1

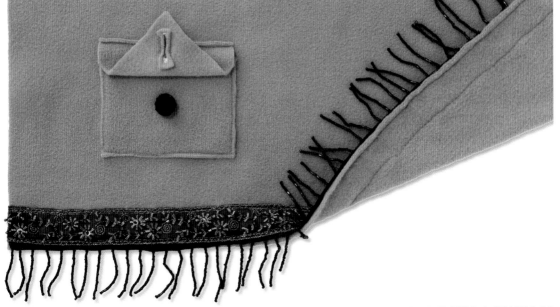

All Buttoned Up

This buttery soft, ginger-colored fleece neck warmer is oh-so-sophisticated, yet very easy to create. It's simply a hemmed rectangle with a three-button closure. Cut the rectangle size to your liking and, for variety, play with trim or closure options. You can also make a sporty version to wear on the slopes.

1 HOUR

Stuff You Need

⅜ yard of 58"–60" medium- or heavyweight fleece

3 buttons (ours are 1⅜" in diameter)

Non-fusible interfacing or other buttonhole reinforcement

Matching or contrasting polyester thread

What You'll Do

Cut out and hem a rectangle

Make buttonholes

Sew on buttons

Our finished size: 9" x 23"

MAKE IT!

1. *Cut it out.* Using a rotary cutter, straight edge, and cutting mat (*see page* 19), cut a 10" x 24" rectangle. Before proceeding, wrap the fabric around your neck to see if this size suits you. Trim as needed.

2. *Hem it.* Hem the neck warmer by turning under all four edges by about ½" and topstitching the edges in place.

3. *Make buttonholes.* Stitch three buttonholes perpendicular to the 10" side of the neck warmer, about 1¾" from the outside edge. Reinforce the buttonhole on the wrong side with non-fusible interfacing or a scrap of fabric. (*See page* 29.)

4. *Attach the buttons.* Hand sew the three buttons in place.

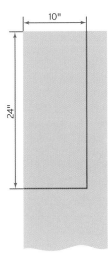

STEP 1

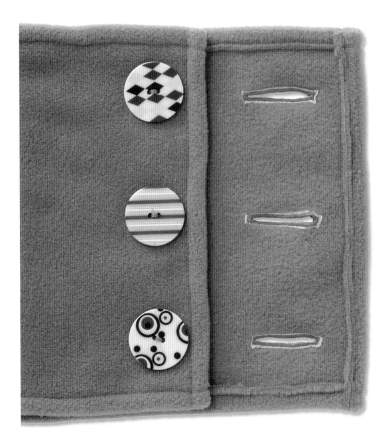

DO IT YOUR WAY

The creative possibilities are endless, but here are a couple of ideas you could try:

- Instead of hemming the raw edges, clip them with pinking shears for a decorative edge.

- For a buttoned look without the buttonholes, sew the buttons on as usual, but use hook-and-loop strips (Velcro) to hold the sides together.

The Cat's Meow

See it. Sew it. Wear it. Dude, bring your personality to the slopes! This headband is so easy you can finish it in the time it takes for a few runs down the mountain.

Stuff You Need

¼ yard of 58"-60" medium-weight fleece

¼ yard of ⅝" grosgrain ribbon

One cat appliqué

Matching or contrasting polyester thread

What You'll Do

Measure your head

Cut out the headband

Stitch it

Embellish it

Our finished size: 3" wide x 26" circumference

MAKE IT!

1. *Measure your head.* Wrap a tape measure snugly around your head in the direction you will wear your headband. Fill in the blanks:

Head measurement = _____" + 1" seam allowance = _____"

2. *Cut it out.* Using a rotary cutter, straight edge, and cutting mat (*see page* 19), cut a strip of fleece that is 6½" wide and the length of the above measurement. ***Very important***: Be sure to cut the ***length*** of the strip in the direction with the greatest ***stretch***.

3. *Stitch the ends.* With right sides together, put the ends together and stitch a ½" seam. Finger-press the seam open. You now have a circle.

4. *Pin and stitch the lengthwise edge*. Fold the strip in half with wrong sides together and right sides out. Line up the lengthwise edges with one side ½" away from the other side. Fold the ½" edge over the top of the other edge and pin it all the way around the head-band. Measure the width of the headband at a few places to keep it consistent at 3". Topstitch the overlapping edge in place. If you want the appearance of the sides to match, also stitch the lengthwise *folded* edge. **Note:** Stitches along the length can reduce the stretchi-ness of the band or may break as the headband stretches. It works better to use a zigzag stitch, even if the zigzag is narrow enough to appear nearly straight.

5. *Embellish.* Wrap the ribbon around the headband at the seamline and stitch it in place. On one side of headband, stitch the cat appliqué in the center of the ribbon.

6½"

head measurement + 1"

STEP 2

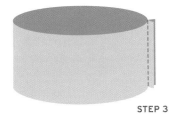

STEP 3

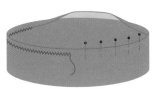

STEP 4

HEADBAND VARIATION

So Many Choices!

With such a wide selection of fleece available, you're sure to find one that makes just the right statement. A bold print like this doesn't need embellish-ment, which means you can make the headband in about 15 minutes!

Eskimo Retro

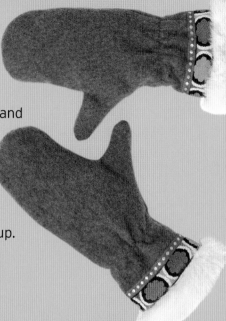

Decorative ribbons and a faux fur trim add personality and flair to this stylish scarf and mitten set. The easy-to-make scarf is double-thickness for extra warmth, and the mittens are custom cut. If fur isn't your style, there are plenty of cuff options: crocheted edging, bias binding, or anything else you can dream up.

Stuff You Need

(for both scarf and mittens)

1 yard of 58"–60" medium-weight fleece

1⅛ yard of 1" embroidered ribbon

1⅝" yard of ⅜" grosgrain ribbon

⅝ yard of faux fur trim

½ yard of ½" elastic

Matching or contrasting polyester thread

What You'll Do

Cut out, stitch, and embellish your scarf

Draw a mitten pattern

Cut out and embellish the mittens

Stitch the elastic and sides

Our finished scarf size: 7" x 50"

Our finished mitten size: 7" x 12"

MAKE THE SCARF

1. *Cut it out.* Using a rotary cutter, straight edge, and cutting mat (*see page* 19), cut a 15" x 51" rectangle. If you decide to make a wider scarf, check that you have enough fabric and ribbon for embellishment.

2. *Stitch it.* Fold the scarf with right sides together, lengthwise. Stitch the raw edges together using a ½" seam allowance. Leave a 3"-wide opening for turning. Clip the corners and turn the scarf right sides out. Hand-sew the opening closed.

STEP 2

STEP 1

3. *Embellish it.* Choose one side of the scarf to embellish with ribbons. Cut the 1" wide ribbon into two 8" pieces and cut the narrow ribbon into four 8" pieces. Position them as shown about 4" away from the ends of the scarf, with the narrow ribbon overlapping the wide ribbon by about ⅛". Turn under the raw ends of each ribbon piece and pin or baste them in place. Stitch through all layers along both sides of each narrow ribbon.

Note: If the ribbons are sliding around too much, baste the wide ribbon in place first, then pin and stitch the narrow ones.

MAKE THE MITTENS

1. *Draw the pattern.* Place your hand on a piece of paper, with your fingers slightly apart. Using a pencil, trace a mitten shape around your hand, allowing about ½" of space between the pencil line and your fingers. Draw a cutting line ½" away from the traced line. Draw a line at the wrist bone, to mark the where the elastic will go. Draw the length of the mitten as desired (ours extends about 3" past the wrist bone) and add ½" for seam allowance.

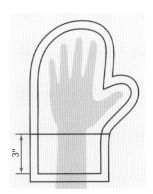

STEP 1

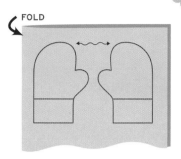

FOLD

STEP 2

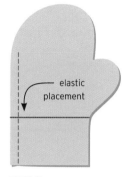

elastic placement

STEP 3

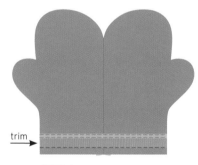

trim

STEP 4

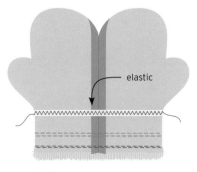

elastic

STEP 5

2. *Cut the fleece.* On a cutting surface, fold a section of fleece with right sides together. Make sure that the direction of greatest stretch runs horizontally. Use the pattern to cut out a total of four mitten pieces: two for the right hand and two for the left. With chalk or a fabric marker, mark the elastic placement line on the wrong side of each mitten piece.

3. *Stitch one side.* With right sides together, stitch the outer edge of two mittens pieces as shown using a ½" seam allowance. End about 4" to 5" above the elastic placement line. Repeat for the second mitten, then open both mittens flat and finger-press the seam allowances open.

4. *Embellish.* Cut both the wide ribbon and the narrow ribbon into two pieces. *For each mitten:* Pin the wide ribbon ½" away from the hem and pin the narrow ribbon above it, overlapping by about ⅛". Stitch along the length of the ribbons. Cut the faux fur trim into two pieces and place its seam edge beneath the mitten edge. Stitch through all layers (ribbon, fleece, and fur edge) twice with seams about ¼" apart.

5. *Stitch the elastic.* On the wrong side of each mitten, measure the width of the elastic placement line. Subtract one inch and cut two pieces of elastic to this length. Pin each end of the elastic to a mitten seam allowance and hold the elastic taut while you zigzag it in place.

6. *Finish the side seams.* Fold each mitten in half, with right sides together. Stitch through all layers around each mitten's edges. Clip the seam allowances of all curves and turn the mittens right sides out. (*See page* 27.)

Purrfect Paws

For a charming way to keep in warmth and keep out the wind, try these fur-trimmed beauties. For a custom fit around your wrist, adjust the elastic cording with a handy toggle. For a different look, the casing can be sewn on the outside of the mitten and embellished.

1 HOUR

Stuff You Need

½ yard of 58"-60" medium-weight fleece

⅝ yard of faux fur trim

¾ yard of elastic cording

2 barrel-lock toggles

Matching or contrasting polyester thread

What You'll Do

Draw a pattern

Cut it out

Make the casing

Stitch it together

Embellish with fur

Our finished size: about 7" x 11"

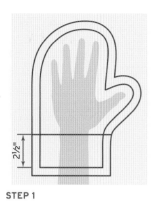

STEP 1

2½"

MAKE IT!

1. Draw the pattern. Follow the instructions for the *Eskimo Retro* mittens pattern. (*See page* 45.) The only difference is the length of the cuff (ours is 2½"), but make yours whatever length you like.

2. Cut the fleece. On a cutting surface, fold a section of fleece with right sides together. Make sure that the direction of greatest stretch runs horizontally. Use the pattern to cut out a total of four mitten pieces: two for the right hand and two for the left. With chalk or a fabric marker, mark the elastic placement line on the wrong side of each mitten piece. For the elastic casing, cut four strips of fleece that are 1" wide and the same length as the mitten's elastic placement line.

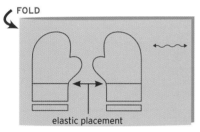

FOLD

elastic placement

STEP 2

3. Make the casing. On a flat surface, place the mittens wrong side up with the thumbs facing to the outside. Stitch the upper edge of each casing strip to each mitten piece, keeping the ends open. Cut the elastic cording into two pieces of equal length (about 14"). *For each mitten:* slip the cording under the casing and secure each end below the thumbs. Pin the casing over the cording and stitch the lower edge of the casing, keeping the elastic free.

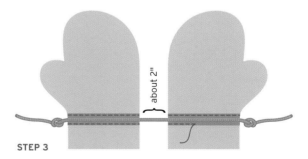

about 2"

STEP 3

4. Stitch it together. Place each of the mittens right sides together and pin. Stitch the mittens together, leaving an opening for the cording. Trim off the knotted ends of the cording, clip the seam allowances, and turn the mittens right sides out. Pull the elastic to the outside and thread the looped end through the toggle.

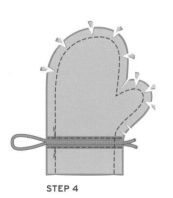

STEP 4

5. Embellish the hem. Hand-sew the black fur trim to each mitten's hemline.

Plush Plaid

Made with a "high loft" fleece, this wintry ensemble has the delicious softness of rabbit fur. And here's a bonus: You can't make a mistake with this fleece. The fleece's pile is so thick and plush that crooked stitching and other sewing "errors" simply disappear!

1 HOUR

Stuff You Need

(for both scarf and hat)

⅝ yard of 58"-60" plaid high loft fleece

⅝ yard of 58"-60" white high loft fleece

2 buttons, 1¼" diameter

Matching or contrasting polyester thread

What You'll Do

Cut out and stitch the scarf

Sew a button (buttonhole optional)

Measure your head

Cut out the hat

Shape and stitch the crown

Hem the hat and add a button

Our finished scarf size: 9" x 50"

Our finished hat size: 7" x 28" around

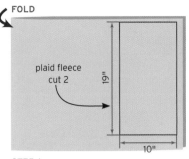

STEP 1

STEP 1

MAKE THE SCARF

1. *Cut it out.* Using a rotary cutter, straight edge, and cutting mat (*see page* 19), cut two 19" x 10" rectangles from the plaid fleece (leftover fleece will be used for the hat) and one 19" x 33" rectangle from the white fleece.

2. *Stitch it up.* With right sides together, stitch the 19" side of a plaid rectangle to each of the 19" sides of the white rectangle. Finger-press the seam allowances open. With right sides together, fold the scarf in half lengthwise and stitch the raw edges together, leaving a 3"-wide opening for turning. Clip the corners and turn the scarf right sides out. Hand-sew the opening closed.

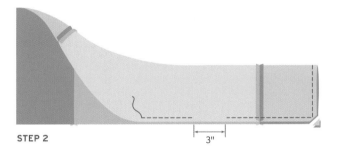

STEP 2

3. *Add a button.* If you'd like to fasten the scarf in place, wrap it around you, cross the ends, and pin it. Hand-sew a button to the scarf, sewing through all layers. If you prefer, make a buttonhole on one side, reinforcing it on the wrong side with non-fusible interfacing or a scrap of fabric. (*See page* 29.) Sew the button on the other side of the scarf.

MAKE THE HAT

1. *Take measurements*. To figure out how big to make your hat, measure your head in two places. For the circumference (A), measure around your head just above your ears. For the length of the hat (B), measure from the top of your head to the bottom of your ear. Then do the math below:

A = ____" + ½" ease + 1" seam allowance = ____"

B = ____" + ½" seam allowance + 1¼" hem allowance = ____"

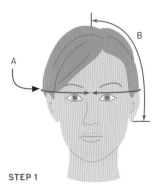

STEP 1

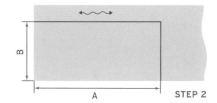

STEP 2

2. Cut out the hat. Lay the plaid fleece on a cutting surface with the greatest stretch running horizontally. Using a rotary cutter and straight edge (*see page* 19), cut a rectangle with the length equal to measurement A and the width equal to measurement B.

3. Stitch the side seam. With right sides together, fold your fabric in half and stitch on the B side of the rectangle.

STEP 3

4. Shape the crown. Fold the fabric in half again, lining up the fabric's foldline with the side seam stitching line. With chalk or a fabric marker, draw an arc that is 3" deep on the sides and meets at the fabric's center point. Sketch an arc that matches both sides. Cut the fleece through all layers on the arc line.

5. Stitch the outer crown. Open out your hat fabric piece and pin the crown pieces together. To sew a smoothly shaped seam without backstitching, use a normal stitch length for most of the seam, then change to a short stitch ½" away from the fold or seam line. Stitch off the edge and cut the threads, leaving a tail about 3" long.

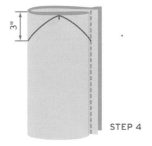

STEP 4

6. Finish the crown. With right sides together, fold the hat in half again. Align the crown shapes together and pin them in place. Stitch the crown seam and taper off the curved edge as in step 5.

7. Hem it. Along the hemline, fold under about 1¼" of fabric to the hat's wrong side. Stitching close to raw edge, zigzag the hem in place. Turn the hat right side out.

8. Sew on a button. Put on the hat and try the seams in different positions to decide how the hat looks best on your head. Pinpoint where to put the button, then sew it on 1¼" above hemline.

INSIDE VIEW

STEP 5

Cupcake

This sweet variation on the plaid hat is a piece of cake to sew. This time you'll cut the hemline extra long to allow for a double-fold edge. Personalize your hat with an appliqué you like and a hand-made fleece tassel. Try it with a solid or print fleece and make up your own whimsical tassel using yarn, beads, or cording.

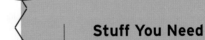

Stuff You Need

⅝ yard of 58"-60" medium-weight fleece

One embroidered appliqué

Matching or contrasting polyester thread

What You'll Do

Create your personal hat pattern

Cut and stitch your hat

Our finished size: 7" x 24" around

MAKE IT!

1. *Take measurements.* To figure out how big to make your hat, measure your head in two places. (*See page* 50.) Then do the math below:

A = ____" + ½" ease + 1" seam allowance = ____"

B = ____" + ½" seam allowance + 8" cuff allowance = ____"

2. *Cut out the hat.* Lay the fleece on a cutting surface with the greatest stretch running horizontally. Using a rotary cutter and straight edge (*see page* 19), cut a rectangle with the length equal to measurement A and the width equal to measurement B. For the tassel, cut two strips of fleece 10" x ⅜" each.

3. *Stitch the side seam and shape the crown.* With right sides together, fold your fabric in half and stitch on the B side of the rectangle. Follow the instructions for step 4 on page 51 to shape the crown.

4. *Stitch the outer crown.* Open out your hat fabric piece and pin the crown pieces together. Stitch the crown along the outer arcs only.

5. *Make the tassels.* Pull on the 10" strips to make tassels. (*See page* 16.) Fold each strip in half to make a four-stranded tassel.

6. *Finish the crown.* Refold the hat in half with right sides together, aligning the side seams and crown. Match the crown seams and pin the folded ends of the tassels to the crown with the tassels *inside* (on the right side) of the hat. Stitch the crown seam through all layers.

7. *Hem it.* Fold and pin 5" of fabric to the hat's wrong side along the hemline and zigzag in place close to the raw edge. Turn the hat right side out. Check for fit, and stitch on your appliqué of choice.

tassel ends

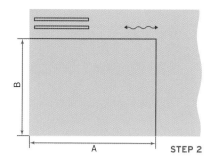

B

A

STEP 2

3"

STEP 3

cuff fold line

5"

STEP 4

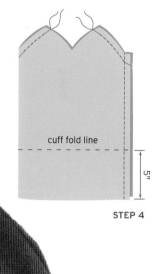

Material Girl Gauntlets

If you are a material girl living in a fleece world, you will definitely need these gauntlet-style hand warmers. You can be stylish, warm, and nimble at the same time. Hip waffle fleece is accented with crocheted trim and antique jet-black buttons. You don't know how to crochet? No problem, this trim is store-bought.

Stuff You Need

³⁄₈ yard of 58"–60" waffle fleece

⁵⁄₈ yard of crocheted trim, 1" wide

3 buttons, ½" diameter

Matching or contrasting polyester thread

What You'll Do

Take measurements

Cut out the gauntlets

Stitch the sides

Embellish as you like

Our finished size: 4" x 9½"

material girl gauntlets

MAKE IT!

1. *Take measurements.* Measure around your hand, just below the base of your fingers. Then measure from your finger knuckles to wherever you want the gauntlets to end. Fill in the blanks:

A = _____" ÷ 2 = _____" + 1" seam allowance + ½" ease = _____"

B = _____" + 2" for hems

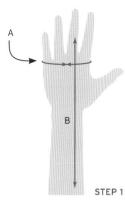

STEP 1

2. *Cut it out.* Using a rotary cutter, straight edge, and cutting mat (*see page* 19), cut four rectangles based on your A and B measurements. Make sure that the greatest stretch runs horizontally across your hands (making it easier to slip them on and off). You can fold the fabric and cut two at a time, but fleece is often easier to cut one layer at a time.

thumb opening

STEP 2

3. *Stitch the thumb-side seams.* Place two of the fabric pieces right sides together. Place them on your arm where you will be wearing them, taking into account the ½" hem at top and bottom. On one of the long sides, mark with chalk where the opening should be for the thumb. Stitch that side, with a backtack on either side of the thumb opening. Match the placement of the thumb opening as you sew the second gauntlet.

STEP 3

4. *Finish the side seams.* Finger-press the thumb-side seam allowances open and topstitch them in place ¼" away from seam. With right sides together, stitch the remaining side seam using a ½" seam allowance.

thumb opening

STEP 4

5. *Hem the ends.* Turn the ends under ½" and stitch them in place.

6. *Embellish.* To decorate the hem of your gauntlets, hand-sew crocheted lace along hem's right side. Hand-sew three buttons along outer side seam, beginning 1" away from crocheted trim.

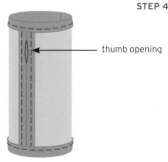

thumb opening

STEP 5

Flashdance Flashback

The eighties called — they want their leg warmers back, so you'll just have to make your own pair! These supersoft leg warmers can be worn thigh high or scrunched at the knee for style and warmth. An elastic casing holds them in place at the top. Add crocheted lace along the hemline or personalize to your taste.

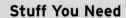

1 HOUR

Stuff You Need

1 yard of 58"-60" medium-weight fleece

¾ yard crocheted lace trim, 1" wide

1 yard of elastic, ⅝" wide

Matching or contrasting polyester thread

What You'll Do

Take measurements

Draw and cut the pattern shape

Embellish with trim

Stitch the sides

Make a casing and add the elastic

Finished size: about 7" x 27"

MAKE IT!

1. *Measure your leg.* Make your leg warmers based on three measurements: your mid thigh, your ankle, and the distance between them. Add 1" to 2" of *ease* (breathing room) as you like. Use the following formula to plot your pattern.

A. Mid thigh = ____ + 1" seam allowance + 1" to 2" ease = ____ "

B. Mid thigh to ankle = ____ + 2" for casings = ____ "

C. Ankle = ____ + 1" seam allowance + 2" to 3" ease = ____ "

2. *Draw the pattern and cut it out.* Using the A, B, and C measurements as shown, plot your leg warmers by drawing directly on the fleece with a chalk marker or by making a paper pattern. Fold the fleece as shown and cut two leg warmers along the folds. *Note:* Use half of A and C because of the fold.

3. *Add trim.* Position a strip of crocheted lace trim along the ankle edge and zigzag stitch it in place.

4. *Stitch the sides.* With right sides together, stitch a ½" seam along the sides of each leg warmer.

5. *Make a casing.* For each leg warmer: Fold the top edge 1" to the inside and topstitch ¾" from the fold, leaving a 2" opening for the elastic. Cut elastic long enough to go around your thigh and thread it through the casing with a safety pin. Try the warmer on to adjust the fit and the elastic length. Then pull the elastic out far enough to stitch the ends in place, backtacking a few times to secure the elastic. Stitch the casing opening closed.

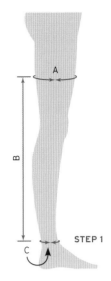

STEP 1

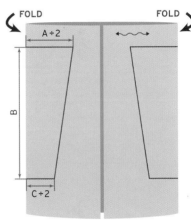

STEP 2

STEP 5

F

LEECE WAS ORIGINALLY DEVELOPED as a high-performance fabric for extreme outdoor sports and activities. Luckily you don't have to be an extremist to enjoy fleece. With the variety of fabric weights, textures, prints, colors, and specialty finishes available in fleece today, you can be warm and fashionable in any season or climate.

Fleece Out

Wavy Gravy

Peace, man! Be one with your fleece! Groovy waves of color, red corded trim, mohair yarn, and turquoise ceramic beads define this fleece poncho. The secret is a custom cut that allows fabric to drape gracefully from your shoulders. With one simple square of fleece fabric, your poncho options are limitless.

Stuff You Need

1¼ yards of 58"–60" medium-weight or heavyweight fleece

3 yards of ¾" fringed trim

6 ceramic cube buttons, ⅜" wide

24" of mohair yarn

Matching or contrasting polyester thread

What You'll Do

Cut a square

Shape the neckline and shoulders

Hem the edges

Embellish with trim

Our finished size: 29" from shoulder to longest point

STEP 1

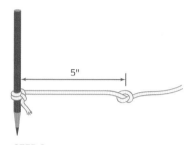

5"

STEP 2

MAKE IT!

1. *Cut it out.* From a single layer of fleece fabric, use a rotary cutter, straight edge, and cutting mat *(see page* 19) to cut a 40" x 40" square. Fold the square into quarters.

2. *Cut the neckline.* To make a round opening for the neckline, trace a quarter circle that extends 5" from the folded corner. If you don't have a compass, tie a piece of string to one end of a chalk pencil or marker and tie a knot 5" away. Put a pin through the knot and into the folded corner of the fabric. Draw an arc from fold to fold, using the chalk and string as a compass. Cut along this line.

3. *Shape the shoulders.* With right sides together, refold the poncho into a triangle by matching opposite corners. For a shapelier fit, trim the shoulder corners as shown below. The angle of this cut is up to you: Have a friend help you pin the poncho shoulders for the best fit and drape. One way to make the sides match is to cut one side, then use the cut piece as a guide for cutting the other side. With the right sides together, stitch the sides of the poncho, ending with a gentle curved seam for your shoulders about 4" away from the neck opening.

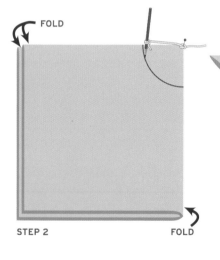

FOLD

STEP 2 FOLD **STEP 3**

END OF THE LiNE

To sew a smoothly shaped seam to the edge of the fabric without backstitching, stitch most of the seam using a normal stitch length, then change to a very short stitch length when you are ½" away from the fold or seam line. Stitch off the edge, knot the threads, and leave a short tail when you cut the threads. If you cut too close to the fabric, the seam may pull open later.

4. *Sew the neckline.* Turn under the neckline edge by ½" and stitch it in place using a narrow zigzag stitch.

5. *Embellish the neckline.* Decorate your poncho any way you like. This one has three beads threaded onto the ends of a 24" length of mohair yarn. The ends are knotted to hold the beads in place. The bow is hand-tacked to the front of the poncho's neckline.

6. *Finish the hem edge.* Pin the fringed trim to the wrong side of the poncho hemline and edgestitch in place.

PONCHO VARIATION

Shagadelic!

It's so easy to customize this poncho, you won't believe it. For instance: Take a rich pumpkin orange, cut the front of the neck into a V-shape, then add a faux fur trim, a striped ribbon, an applique patch — whatever suits your fancy. The result will be your very own one-of-a-kind creation.

Shrug It Off

Take off the chill and welcome spring with this soft buttercup shrug, accented with crocheted flowers. For a custom fit, just sketch and stitch the basic shape, try it on, and cut away the fabric you don't want. For a classic look, keep your fleece unadorned like a beautiful cashmere sweater. For a more retro look, add appliqués, embroidery, beading, or an intriguing brooch.

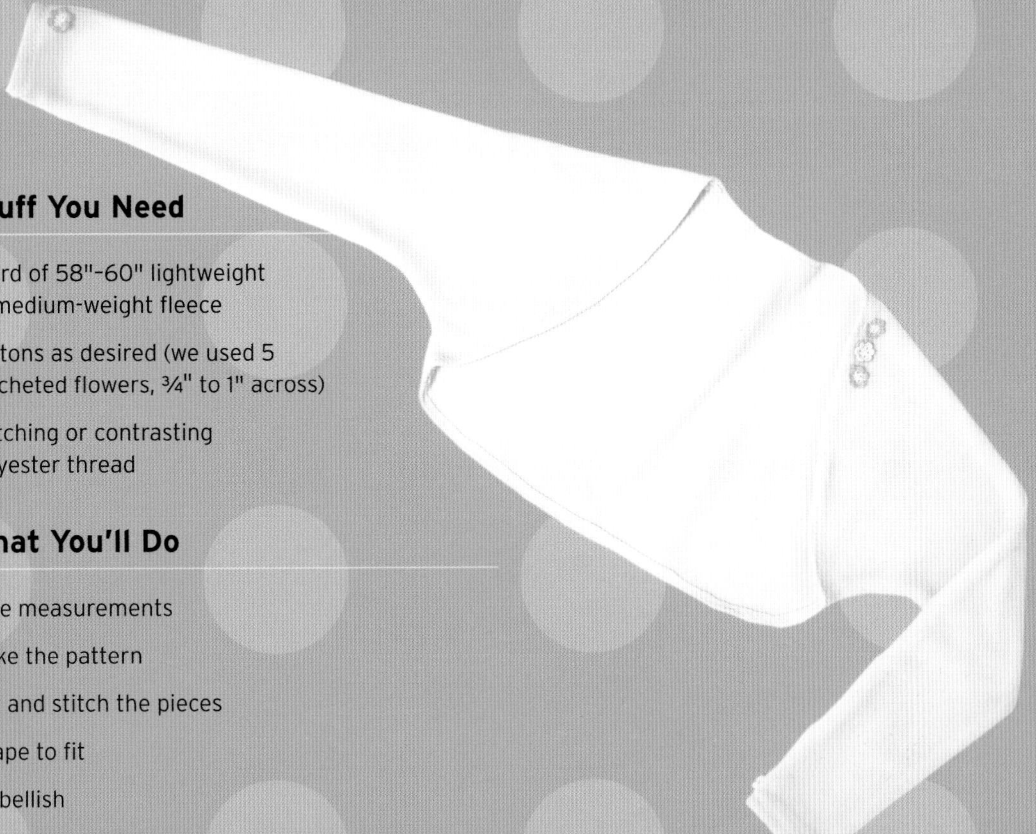

Stuff You Need

1 yard of 58"-60" lightweight or medium-weight fleece

Buttons as desired (we used 5 crocheted flowers, ¾" to 1" across)

Matching or contrasting polyester thread

What You'll Do

Take measurements

Make the pattern

Cut and stitch the pieces

Shape to fit

Embellish

Our finished length: 13½" (in the back)

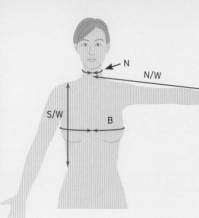

VITAL STATISTICS

To make your shrug, you'll need the following five body measurements:

S/W = _____" *Shoulder to Waist.* The distance from shoulder to waistline.

N/W = _____" *Neck to Wrist.* The distance from mid-neck to wrist bone.

N = _____" *Neck.* The dimension around your neck.

B = _____" *Bust.* The dimension around your bustline.

W = _____" *Wrist.* The dimension around your wrist.

KEEP IT STRAIGHT

When drawing a pattern, it helps to have a right-angle on hand to keep the lines straight. In a pinch, you can use the sides and corners of a book to keep the lines straight and pattern corners square.

MAKE IT!

1. *Do the math.* Use the measurements in Vital Statistics to fill in the blanks below.

A = S/W _____" + 1" for two seam allowances = _____"

B = N/W _____" + 1" ease + ½" seam allowance = _____"

C = N _____" ÷ 4 = _____"

D = B _____" + 1" ease = _____" ÷ 4 = _____" + 1" for seam allowances = _____"

E = S/W _____" ÷ 3 = _____" + ½" seam allowance = _____"

F = W _____" + 2½" ease = _____" ÷ 2 = _____" + 1" for seam allowances = _____"

2. *Draw the pattern.* With a rotary cutter, straight edge, and cutting mat (*see page 19*), fold the fleece in half lengthwise and cut it as long as A. Trim the width as needed to match B. (Or, draw on a sheet of paper that is the size of A x B.) Refer to the diagram as you do the following:

● From the upper left folded corner, measure and mark the C width.

● Mark a spot ½" below the upper left corner and draw a curved line to the C width.

● From the folded lower corner, measure and mark the D width.

● From there, measure up to the E width and draw a straight line.

● Draw a straight line from E to the lower right hand corner.

FOLD

B

C

BACK
cut 1

A

E

F

D

STEP 2

- From there, measure up the side to the F width.

- Draw a straight line from the F width to the C width.

- Use a right angle to draw a line from the F width to the opposite side of the sleeve.

- Round off the corner at E.

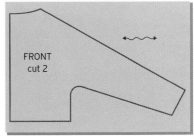

FRONT
cut 2

STEP 3

3. *Cut it out.* Cut out the pattern you just made. (If you drew on paper, position the pattern on the fold, then cut.) This piece is the back of the shrug. Cut two more pieces for the front on the remaining pieces of fleece.

4. *Stitch it up.* With right sides together, pin the shrug fronts to the shrug back. Stitch sleeves and side seams.

5. *Shape it.* Try on the shrug to check the sleeve and underarm fit. If you want a short shrug, adjust the length. Decide how you want the front to curve from the shoulder to the hemline. Draw a curved line with chalk and pin the fabric to test the shape, or cut

STEPS 4 & 5

directly into the fabric. Leave enough fabric to turn under a hem. It helps to cut one side, then match up the two fronts to cut the curve on the other side.

6. *Hem it.* To finish all raw edges, turn them under ½" and zigzag in place.

7. *Embellish.* Hand-sew a button on each sleeve and along the front edges as desired.

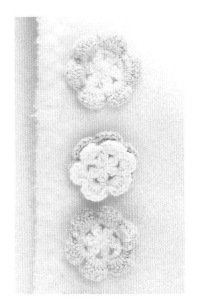

EASE INTO IT

How tightly do you want your shrug to fit? Generally, you want to add ease (a little extra breathing room) to your core measurements, so the shrug isn't too tight. If you're unsure what to add, it's better to cut the shrug larger than you think you'll need and make adjustments later.

Spice Girl

Cinnamon spice and everything nice — that's what this vest is made of. Make yours to suit your needs and style. How long do you want it to be? How roomy? Do you want a hood or not? Let your creativity be the main ingredient. Our vest is designed to be close-fitting, with a zipper, hood, and patch pockets — but feel free to adapt our instructions to make the vest of your dreams. If you're intimidated by zippers, check out the no-zipper variation on page 73.

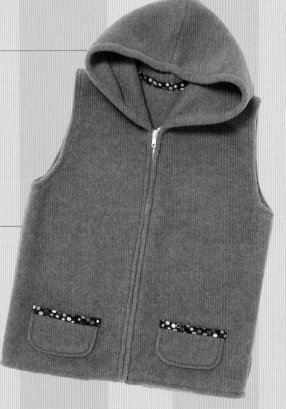

Stuff You Need

1¼ yards of 58"-60" medium
 weight fleece

1 yard of ½" decorative, double-
fold bias binding

1 matching 18"-24"separating zipper*

Matching or contrasting polyester thread

What You'll Do

Make a body template and cutting guide

Cut the fabric

Stitch and shape the vest to fit

Install a zipper

Make and attach the hood

Add pockets

Our finished length: 23"

  *The zipper length depends on your height and how long you
   make the vest. Work out your measurements and pattern
   ideas (steps 1-3) to see what you need.

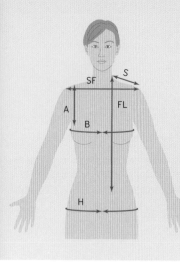

ViTAL STATiSTiCS

To make the vest, you'll need the following body measurements:

S = _____" *Shoulder*. Distance from side of neck to shoulder tip.

SF = _____" *Shoulder front*. The distance from shoulder tip to shoulder tip across the front of your body.

B = _____" *Bust.* The bust measurement around your body.

H = _____" *Hip.* The distance around the fullest part of your hips.

FL = _____" *Front length.* Desired finished length from neck to hemline.

A = _____" *Armhole depth.* Desired finished depth of the armhole.

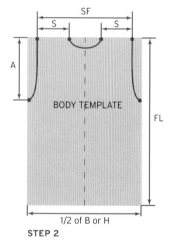

STEP 2

MEASURE AND CUT

1. *Take your measurements.* Ask a friend to help you measure yourself and fill in the blanks under Vital Statistics.

2. *Make a body template.* Drafting a body template is the first step to making clothes that fit you perfectly. See the Body Double box and refer to the diagram as you do the following:

● For the width of the template, use your bust or your hip measurement (whichever is larger) divided by 2.

● For the length, use the FL measurement.

● Draw a line down the center of the template to indicate the center line of the template. Center the SF measurement at the top of the template.

● Plot the S measurements from both sides of the SF measurement.

● Plot the A measurements from each top corner.

● You can draw curved lines for your neck and armhole, but you won't actually shape the fabric until later.

3. *Make a cutting guide.* The next step is to make a guide for cutting the fabric. You will use the body template folded in half, then add allowances for ease, hem, and seams. Here are some pointers:

● Draw the cutting guide on a separate piece of paper (such as brown wrapping paper or the back of some gift wrap). Or, draw chalk lines directly on your fabric (folded with right sides together).

EASE iNTO iT

For a close-fitting vest, adding 1½"-2" ease to the side seams. Or, measure a jacket that fits you well and use that as a guide. If you're unsure, cut the vest larger than you think you'll need and adjust it as you go.

- We added ½" seam allowances to all sides, with an extra 1" on the outside seam for ease.

- Zipper lengths come in even sizes, for instance: 18", 20", 22", 24", and so on. Plan the length of your vest front accordingly (the way you cut the neck will change the front measurement). It's best to cut the vest longer than you think you need and adjust it later to fit.

- Mark where both sides of the shoulder are, as well as the depth of the armholes.

4. Cut out the vest body. Fold the fleece with right sides together and the greatest stretch running horizontally. Cut a block for the vest back along the fold; the seam allowance is not needed for the back, so let the cutting guide overlap the folded edge by ½". Cut another block through two layers for the front pieces. On all three pieces, mark each shoulder and armhole point with a pin.

5. Cut out the hood and pockets. For the hood A measurement, drape a tape measure over your head and measure from your neck on either side. For B, measure around your neck, then do the math below:

A = _____" + 1" ease + 1" for two seam allowances = _____"

B = _____" + 4"-5" for drape + 1" for two seam allowances = _____"

Cut two fabric pieces the size of A x B. For the pockets, cut out two rectangles to your preferred size (ours are 3" x 5" with rounded bottom curves).

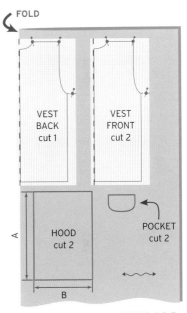

STEPS 4 & 5

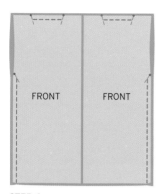

FRONT   FRONT

STEP 6

STEPS 7 & 8

STEP 9

PUT IT TOGETHER

6. *Stitch the side seams.* With right sides together, machine-stitch the front blocks to the back block at the shoulder seams (between the pins) and the side seams (from the armhole pin down to the hem).

7. *Shape the armholes.* Turn the vest right side out and put it on. Check the width and angle of the shoulder seam, the depth of the armhole, and the fit around the hips. Make adjustments as needed. Turn under the fabric at the armhole edges and pin. Take off the vest and check that the sides match. It might help to compare the armhole shape to an existing vest. Topstitch the armhole seams and trim away the excess fabric.

8. *Shape the neckline.* Will your front neckline be rounded or angled like a V? Put on the vest, fold under the fabric at the neckline, and pin it. Take off the vest and check that the neck shape matches on both sides. Take the length of the zipper into consideration, adding ½" for seam allowance at the top and the bottom of the zipper. When you're satisfied that your plan will work, cut the neckline.

9. *Stitch the zipper and hem.* Turn under the center front opening by ½" and baste it in place. Open the zipper into two separate halves and pin the right side of each half to the wrong side of each front edge. Leave a ½" seam allowance at the top and ½" or more at the bottom for the hem. Machine-stitch the zipper in place and remove the basting threads. Turn under the lower hem edge as needed and machine stitch close to raw edge.

10. *Make the hood.* You're almost done! Just a few more steps:

a. Open the vest and measure the width of the neckline (NL). Divide this number by 2, then add 1" for two seam allowances.

NL

STEP 10a

b. Use this measurement to draw a sloped line on the bottom of the hood rectangles. If the hood is too wide, trim off the excess. Draw a curved line that rounds off the upper left corner, then stitch the seam as shown. Turn under the front hem of the hood ½" and topstitch.

c. With right sides together, pin the hood to the neck edge and stitch in place. Trim the seam allowance to ¼". Finger-press the seam open and cover it by pinning and topstitching double-fold bias tape over the seamline. Fold under the raw edges of the bias tape, covering the raw edges of zipper.

11. *Stitch the pockets and hem.* Stitch bias binding to the top edge of each pocket piece, with the raw edges of the binding folded to the wrong side. Stitch the pockets to lower edge of each vest front. (Ours are 2" from the hemmed edges.)

HOOD

NL ÷ 2 + 1"

STEP 10b

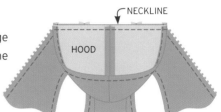

NECKLINE

HOOD

STEP 10c

VEST VARIATION

Barbie's Dream Vest

Okay, so technically this vest isn't made of fleece, but who cares? This show-stopping faux fur vest will turn heads wherever you go. It's easier to make than the zippered hooded vest, although we recommend adding a lining for comfort. Here are a few tips:

- Leave the front open or add a metal clasp, frog closure, or a toggle button.

- Cut and assemble the lining the same as the vest, with one exception. The lining should be a little bit smaller so it doesn't show. Trim away a scant ⅛" from the armholes, neckline, and hemline before sewing it to the vest.

- To attach the lining, pin it and the vest right sides together. Stitch around the outside perimeter (not around the armholes), leaving a gap at the bottom wide enough to turn the attached pieces right sides out. Turn and hand sew any remaining lining edges.

- When sewing with faux fur, test it first to find the best settings. Reduce the presser-foot pressure, lengthen the stitch, and use a narrow zigzag stitch instead of a straight seam. To prevent sliding, use lots of pins and a Teflon-coated or a walking presser foot.

Hot Toddy

Winter white lends this jacket a cool elegance that wears well in any social setting. It features a V-neck and sleeves trimmed with buttons, faux fur, and embroidered ribbon. There are no hems — raw edges are hand-sewn with embroidery floss. This is a great foundation jacket with a wealth of possibilities for variations. Change the neckline depth and shape, change the length, and embellish hems and sleeves as you like.

Stuff You Need

1⅓ yards of 58"-60" medium-weight fleece

⅞ yards of ¾" embroidered ribbon

⅞ yards of 1" faux fur trim

1-2 skeins of embroidery floss
or pearl cotton

5 buttons, 1⅛" diameter

Matching or contrasting polyester
thread

Optional: non-woven interfacing
for buttonhole reinforcement

What You'll Do

Make a body template and cutting guide

Cut the fabric

Stitch and shape the jacket to fit

Embellish the sleeves

Make buttonholes and sew on buttons

Hand-sew the edges

Our finished length: 21"

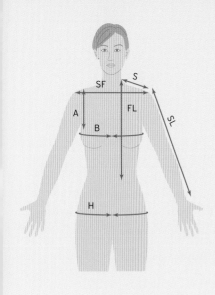

ViTAL STATiSTiCS

To make this jacket and others that follow, you'll need the following measurements:

S = ____" *Shoulder.* Distance from side of neck to shoulder tip.

SF = ____" *Shoulder front.* The distance from shoulder tip to shoulder tip across the front of your body.

B = ____" *Bust.* The bust measurement around your body.

H = ____" *Hip.* The distance around the fullest part of your hips.

FL = ____" *Front length.* Desired length from neck to hemline.

SL = ____" *Sleeve length.* Desired length from shoulder to wrist.

A = ____" *Armhole depth.* Desired finished depth of the armhole.

MEASURE AND CUT

1. *Take your measurements.* Ask a friend to help you measure yourself and fill in the blanks under Vital Statistics. How is this different from the vest? This jacket is meant to be shorter than the vest (although that is up to you) and you'll need your sleeve length.

2. *Make a body template.* Drafting a body template is the first step to making clothes that fit you perfectly. Refer to the diagram as you do the following. (If you've already made a body template for another project, you can use that; just note any differences in the length.)

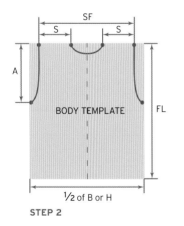

STEP 2

- For the width of the template, use your bust or your hip measurement (whichever is larger) divided by 2.

- For the length, use the FL measurement.

- Draw a line down the center of the template to indicate the center line of the template. Center the SF measurement at the top of the template.

- Plot the S measurements from both sides of the SF measurement.

- Plot the A measurements from each top corner.

- You can draw curved lines for your neck and armhole, but you won't actually shape the fabric until later.

3. *Make a cutting guide.* Cut or fold the body template in half and add allowances for ease, hem, and seams. Here are some pointers:

- Draw the cutting guide on a separate piece of paper (such as brown wrapping paper or the back of some gift wrap). Or, draw chalk lines directly on your fabric (folded with right sides together).

- For our jacket, we added a ½" seam allowance at the top, with no hem added at the bottom. On the left side we added 1½" for the jacket front overlap; on the right we added 2" for ease and ½" for seam allowance. However, add what works for your design.

- If you want to trace the shape of the neck or armhole, you can, but it's not necessary. You will cut the fabric as a block, then later shape it to fit directly on your body. However, do mark where both sides of the shoulder are, as well as the depth of the armhole.

4. *Cut out the jacket body.* Fold the fleece with right sides together and the greatest stretch running horizontally. Cut a block for the jacket back along the fold; the overlap is not needed for the back, so let the cutting guide overlap the folded edge by 1½". Cut another block through two layers for the front pieces. On all three pieces, mark each shoulder and armhole point with a pin.

5. *Cut out the sleeves.* Draw and cut two rectangles based on the following:

A = armhole depth _____" x 2 = _____" + 1" for two seam allowances = _____"

B = sleeve length _____" + 1" for two seam allowances = _____"

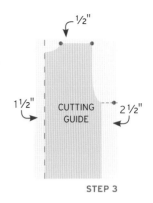

STEP 3

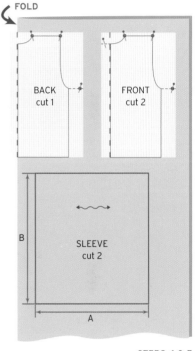

STEPS 4 & 5

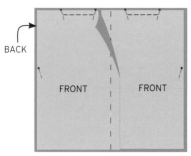

BACK FRONT FRONT

STEP 6

STEP 7

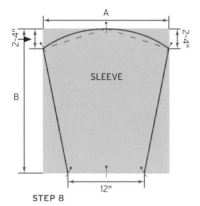

A

2–4"

2–4"

SLEEVE

B

12"

STEP 8

STEP 9

PUT IT TOGETHER

6. *Stitch the shoulders.* With right sides together, machine-stitch the front blocks to the back block at the shoulder seams (between the pins). Mark the armhole depth with a pin or marker.

7. *Shape the jacket.* Turn the jacket right sides out and put it on. Check the width and angle of the shoulder seam, the depth of the armhole, the length, and the amount of overlap in front. Make adjustments as needed. Using the armhole depth as a guide, turn under the fabric at the armhole edges and pin, or mark with chalk where you want to cut. Do the same to make a V at the neckline. Take off the jacket and check that the sides match before cutting the neck and armhole shapes. If you like, round off the lower front corners of the jacket.

8. *Shape the sleeve.* First check that the depth of the armhole is equal to the width of the sleeve fabric block. Fleece is stretchy, so it doesn't have to be exact, just close enough. Shape the top of the sleeve as follows:

- Fold the fabric in half along the A line. Mark both the top and bottom center points with pins or chalk marks.

- Lay the fabric flat, right side down, and measure 2"-4" down from the top edge. Mark the sides of the sleeve with pins or chalk marks.

- With chalk or disappearing marker, draw a straight line from each side mark to the center mark on the A line. Using the straight lines as a guide, draw two gently sloped curves for the top of the sleeve.

- Based on an existing jacket that you like, decide how wide you want the cuff to be and add 1" for seam allowance. (Ours is 11" + 1" = 12".) Center that width on the bottom edge.

- Draw a straight line between marks for each side of the sleeve.

- Once you cut out this sleeve, use it as a guide to cut the other sleeve.

9. *Attach the sleeves.* With right sides together, center the sleeves over the shoulder seam and machine-stitch in place.

10. *Embellish the sleeves.* At the end of the sleeve, pin the faux fur raw edge under the fleece and the embroidered ribbon on top. Stitch through all layers.

11. *Stitch the side seams.* With right sides together, pin the jacket sleeves and side seams together. On each side of the jacket, stitch from cuff to hemline, backtacking at each end.

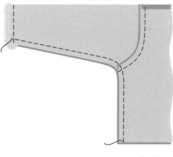

STEP 11

12. *Make the buttonholes.* Make five buttonholes on the jacket right front, to the width of your buttons of choice. Reinforce the buttonhole on the wrong side with non-fusible interfacing or a scrap of fabric. (*See page* 29.) Cut open the buttonholes and hand-sew the buttons onto the jacket left front. If you wish, add buttons to the sleeves as decoration.

13. *Finish the jacket.* Using embroidery floss or other finishing thread, hand-sew a blanket stitch around the jacket front, back and hemline.

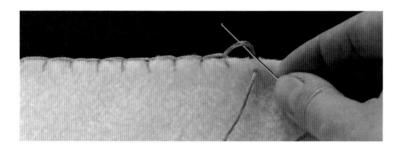

JACKET VARIATION

Posh Puff

This cozy blond jacket could easily become your favorite. Curly fleece — which is wavy on one side and furry on the other — is a natural for turned-back collars, hemlines, and cuffs. Simply fold over the edge 1" to 2" and hand-sew. Instant embellishment! With a finished length of 33", this jacket was made from 1²/₃ yards of fleece. The V-neck was cut a bit deeper and an extra strip of shaped and folded fleece was added to the neckline edge. Three elegant snaps were used instead of buttons, and the finished sleeve opening is 14" instead of 11". For additional walking ease, an 8" slit was cut in the center back.

Babydoll

Not your run-of-the-mill timberland jacket, this plaid creation has babydoll innocence and grownup sophistication. Brocade godets with Chinese frogs dress up the sleeves. Thanks to the nature of fleece — which won't ravel — there are no hems or facings, only neatly cut edges. Lengthen or shorten the jacket bodice, add more (or less) fullness to the gathers, or change the neckline and collar shape, whatever you like.

Stuff You Need

1½ yards of 58"-60" medium-weight plaid fleece

⅜ yard of 44" brocade fabric

2 Chinese frog closures

3 buttons, 1⅛" diameter

Matching or contrasting polyester thread

Optional: non-woven interfacing for buttonhole reinforcement

What You'll Do

Make a body template and cutting guide

Cut the fabric

Shape the sleeves and make the godet

Stitch and shape the jacket to fit

Gather and attach the peplum

Make buttonholes and sew on buttons

Hand-sew the edges

Our finished length: 26"

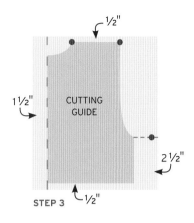

½"

1½"

CUTTING
GUIDE

2½"

½"

STEP 3

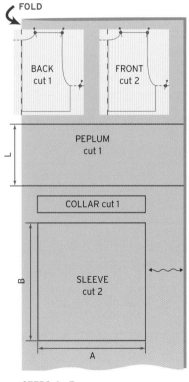

FOLD

BACK
cut 1

FRONT
cut 2

PEPLUM
cut 1

L

COLLAR cut 1

SLEEVE
cut 2

B

A

STEPS 4 - 7

MEASURE AND CUT

1. *Take your measurements.* Ask a friend to help you measure yourself and fill in the blanks under Vital Statistics on page 76.

2. *Make a body template.* Draft a body template as instructed on page 76. If you've already made one, then you're all set.

3. *Make a cutting guide.* Add allowances for ease, hem, and seams to make a cutting guide for the fabric. Here are some pointers:

- Draw the cutting guide on a piece of paper or draw chalk lines directly on your fabric (folded with right sides together).

- Measure for the upper portion of the jacket by measuring from your shoulder to the point below your breast where you want the peplum to start. Our jacket top is 14".

- For this jacket, we added 1" for seam allowances at both top and bottom. On the left side we added 1½" for the jacket overlap; on the right we added 2" for ease plus ½" for seam allowance.

- If you want to trace the shape of the neck or armhole, you can, but it's not necessary. However, do mark where both sides of the shoulder are, as well as the depth of the armhole.

4. *Cut out the jacket body.* Fold the fleece with right sides together and the greatest stretch running horizontally. Cut a block for the jacket back along the fold; the overlap is not needed for the back, so let the cutting guide overlap the folded edge by 1½". Cut another block through two layers for the front pieces. On all three pieces, mark each shoulder and armhole point with a pin.

5. *Cut out the peplum.* For the length (L), decide how long you want the peplum to be (ours is 12"), then add ½" for one seam allowance. Ours has no hem along the bottom, but if you want one, add another ½" to 1". The width depends on your measurements and how gathered you want the peplum to be. For fleece, the gathered edge should be about 1½ times the length of the edge you are sewing it to. Most likely the full width of a 60" fleece will work just fine. If the gathers get too bulky, use less length.

6. *Cut out the collar.* Let's keep this simple. Cut a strip that is 3" wide and at least 22" or more long. Later you can cut it to fit.

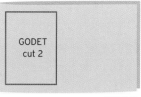

GODET
cut 2

STEP 8

7. Cut out the sleeve blocks. Draw and cut two rectangles based on the following:

A = armhole depth _____" x 2 = _____" + 1" for two seam allowances = _____"

B = sleeve length _____" + 1" for two seam allowances = _____"

8. Cut out the godet block. Again, let's keep this simple. Cut a 8" x 11 ½" rectangle from the brocade fabric.

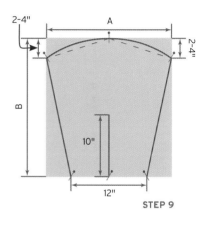

STEP 9

PUT IT TOGETHER

9. Shape the sleeve. Refer to the instructions on page 78 for shaping the sleeve. The only difference for this sleeve is the cut for the godet; from the center pin at the bottom of the sleeve, measure and cut a slash that is 10" long.

10. Stitch the sleeve godet. With right sides up, open and pin the slashed sleeve to the godet fabric block. Machine-stitch the V-opening close to the raw edge of the fleece. On the wrong side, trim away excess satin fabric along the sides of the V, and finish the seam allowance with zigzag stitching or pinked edges. At the hemline, turn under the raw edge of the godet twice, and topstitch across the sleeve. If you like, stitch around the entire sleeve, which will keep it from stretching too much. As an option, hand-sew a frog to the right side of the sleeve at the top of the godet.

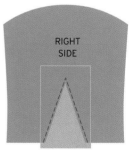

RIGHT
SIDE

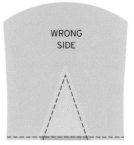

WRONG
SIDE

STEP 10

HOT SPOT

The top of the godet is an ideal spot for a bit of decoration.

11. *Stitch the shoulders.* With right sides together, pin the jacket body blocks together and stitch the shoulder seams together between the pins. Mark the armhole depth with a pin or marker.

12. *Shape the jacket top.* Turn the jacket right sides out and put it on. Check the width and angle of the shoulder seam, the depth of the armhole, the length, and the amount of overlap in front. Make adjustments as needed. Using the armhole depth as a guide, turn under the fabric at the armhole edges and pin, or mark with chalk where you want to cut. Do the same to make a rounded neckline. Take off the jacket and check that the sides match before cutting the neck and armhole shapes.

13. *Stitch the sleeves at the shoulder.* With right sides together, center the sleeves over the shoulder seam and machine-stitch in place.

14. *Stitch the side seams.* With right sides together, pin the jacket sleeves and side seams together. On each side of the jacket, stitch from cuff to the peplum edge, backtacking at each end.

15. *Baste the peplum.* Fold the peplum in half lengthwise to find its center, then mark the spot with a pin or marker. From one end to the other, machine-baste two parallel rows of stitching near the top edge of the peplum.

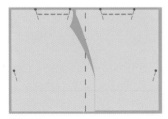

STEP 11

STEP 12

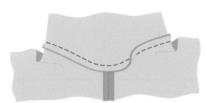

STEP 13

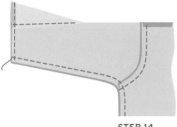

STEP 14

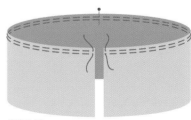

STEP 15

16. *Stitch the peplum to the jacket.* Line up the center of the peplum with the center of the back of the jacket and pin the two, right sides together. Also pin both ends of the peplum to the jacket. Evenly gather the peplum along the basting stitches to fit the width of the jacket, pinning often. Machine-stitch.

17. *Attach the collar.* Pin the right side of the collar fabric to the wrong side of the jacket neckline and machine stitch in place. Trim the seam allowance to ¼" and trim away excess collar fabric. A semicircle of brocade frabric stitched to the back of the neck adds a classy "designer" look.

18. *Make the buttonholes.* Make three buttonholes on the right jacket front. Reinforce the buttonholes with non-woven, non-fusible interfacing or an extra layer of fleece fabric. (*See page* 29.) Cut open the buttonholes and hand-sew the buttons to the jacket left front.

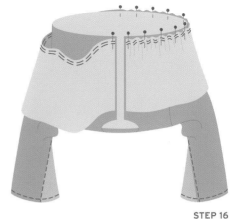

STEP 16

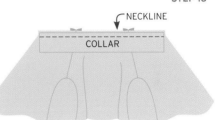

NECKLINE

COLLAR

STEP 17

City Slicker

When you start with fabric like this, you can't go wrong! This lightweight fleece features flowers and paisley patterns, machine-embroidered with sequins and gold metallic thread. Artfully placed vintage buttons and fancy embroidered ribbon at the cuffs add just the right touch. Everything you need to know to make this coat is already in this chapter, but we'll walk you through some hints and reminders.

Stuff You Need

1½ yards of 58"-60" embroidered fleece

A selection of ¾" to 1⅛" vintage buttons

⅔ yard of organza ribbon, 2" wide

Matching or contrasting polyester thread

What You'll Do

Make a body template and cutting guide

Cut the fabric

Stitch and shape the coat to fit

Shape, stitch, and embellish the sleeves

Add a collar

Make buttonholes and sew on buttons

Our finished length: 41"

MAKE IT!

1. *Take your measurements and make a body template.* Fill in your Vital Statistics and follow the instructions on page 76. For the front length, measure from neck to knee.

2. *Make a cutting guide.* Refer to the pointers on page 77 for making a cutting guide. Our adjustments for this project are as follows:

- Top: ½" seam allowance; bottom ½" hem
- Left side: 4" for a folded overlap
- Right side: 2" ease + ½" seam allowance.

3. *Cut out the pieces.* Fold the fleece with right sides together and the greatest stretch running horizontally. Cut out the pieces as indicated. The overlap is not needed for the back, so let the cutting guide overlap the folded edge by 4". For a folded collar, cut a strip that is 5" wide and at least 20" or more long. To figure out the size of the sleeve block, see page 77.

4. *Stitch the shoulder seams.* With right sides together, machine stitch the front blocks to the back block at the shoulder seams (between the pins). Try on the coat and shape the neck and armholes. (*See page* 78.) Fold under both of the front overlaps (where the buttons and buttonholes will be) by about 2" and stitch in place.

5. *Shape the sleeves.* Follow instructions for shaping the sleeves and sew them to the coat. (*See page* 78.) Embellish the cuffs.

6. *Stitch the side seams.* See page 79.

7. *Attach the collar.* With right sides together, pin the collar fabric to the jacket neckline and machine-stitch. Finger-press the seam allowance toward the collar, then fold the collar in half, wrong sides together. Stitch the collar to the seam allowance and hand-sew the ends.

8. *Make the buttonholes.* Place the buttons and make buttonholes as desired. (*See page* 29.) Experiment with button sizes and placement.

9. *Optional slits and hems.* If you like, measure and cut a 12" walking slit in the center of the coat back. Stitch along the edge for reinforcement, and hem the coat bottom and sleeves for a more finished look.

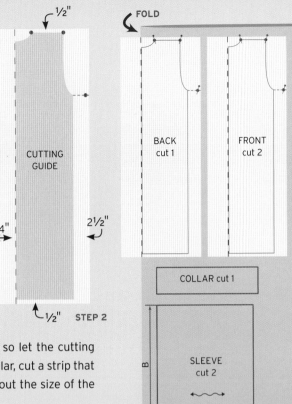

½"

CUTTING GUIDE

4"

2½"

½"   **STEP 2**

FOLD

BACK cut 1

FRONT cut 2

COLLAR cut 1

SLEEVE cut 2

B

A

STEP 3

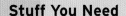

War and Fleece

Stand out in camo-print fleece! This is one outfit that won't leave you blending in with the crowd. Metal grommet detailing adds to the texture and visual interest, as does the waffle-fleece ruffle and side pocket. An optional godet in back adds extra fullness. You can add more snaps and grommets, or omit them all for an easy-to-sew A-line skirt.

Stuff You Need

2 yards of 58"–60" camouflage print medium-weight fleece

¾ yard of 58"–60" solid color waffle fleece

1 yard of ¾" twill tape with grommets

1 matching 7" zipper

Matching or contrasting polyester thread

Optional:

⅜" snaps and setter

½" grommets and setter

What You'll Do

Take measurements

Draw the pattern

Cut and stitch the fleece

Install a zipper

Add a back seam godet (optional)

Make a pocket and a ruffle

Embellish as you like

Our finished length: 30"

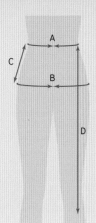

VITAL STATISTICS

To make an A-line skirt with a fitted waistline, you need the following measurements:

A = Waist ____" + 2" for seam allowances + 1"-2" ease = ____" ÷ 4 = ____"

B = Hips ____" + 2" for seam allowances + 2" to 4" ease = ____"÷ 4 = ____"

C = Waist to hips ____"

D = Desired length ____" minus 2½" for the ruffle = ____"

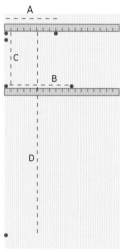

STEP 2

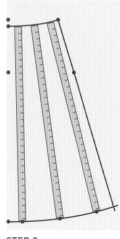

STEP 3

MEASURE AND CUT

1. *Take measurements.* Fill in the measurements in Vital Statistics on this page.

2. *Plot the pattern points.* Plan your skirt by drawing directly on folded fabric or by making a custom paper pattern that you can use again later. (Another option is to make a pattern from your favorite A-line skirt by tracing the skirt onto paper and adding ½" on all sides for seam allowances.) To start from scratch, here's what you do:

- Near the top, mark a spot for the waistline, then mark ½" to 1" above the first mark (to plot the waistline curve).

- With a ruler, plot a line straight across from the top mark to the A width.

- Mark the distance from waist to hip (C).

- With a ruler, plot a line straight across to mark the B width.

- From the A line, mark the desired length (D).

3. *Make the pattern.* Now that you've marked the key points, connect the dots as follows:

- At the waist, draw a curved line as shown.

- For the side seam, draw a straight line from the waist width to the hip width to the hem length.

- For the hemline, use a yardstick to mark the D measurement from the waistline curve at several points. Connect the points to draw a curve for the hemline.

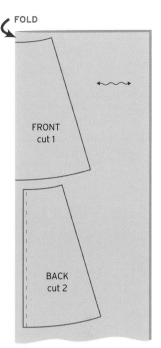

STEP 4

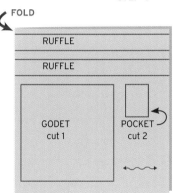

STEP 5

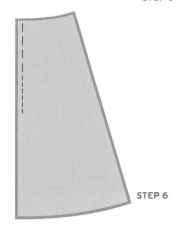

STEP 6

WHERE'S YOUR WAIST?

We usually refer to the top of the skirt as the waistline, but in today's fashion, the top of the skirt can sit anywhere from your actual waistline to your hipline. If you like your skirts to ride below the waist, measure that spot for your waist measurement.

4. Cut out the camouflage fleece. Fold the fleece with right sides together and the greatest stretch running horizontally.

● For the front piece, place the skirt pattern on the fold and cut.

● For the back pieces, move the pattern away from the fold and add ½" seam allowance to the center back seam.

5. Cut out the waffle fleece. Fold the fleece with right sides together and the greatest stretch running horizontally.

● Decide how wide you want the ruffle to be. Ours is 3", and you could certainly try a wider one, but keep the bulkiness of fleece in mind. You don't want to add too much weight to the bottom of the skirt. As for the length, the same consideration applies to a long ruffle that is too heavily gathered. In most cases, two ruffle strips cut to the width of the fabric should work fine. If you want more ruffle or if your fleece is less than 58" wide, cut an additional strip.

● For the skirt pocket and flap, cut out two 4½" x 6" rectangles. You can shape the pocket flap later.

● For the optional godet insert in back, cut one 18" x 18" square.

PUT IT TOGETHER

6. Stitch the zipper and center back seam. If you plan to add a godet to the center back seam, starting stitching 16" up from the skirt hemline; otherwise start at the hemline. As you stitch up the seam, change to a long basting stitch for the upper 8" where the skirt zipper will be sewn. Finger-press the seam allowances open. Pin the zipper face down on the center back seam and stitch in place. (*See page* 30.)

STEP 7

7. *Make the godet.* With right sides up, spread the opening in the skirt back and pin the sides onto the godet fabric block. Machine-stitch the V-opening close to the raw edge of the fleece; make a point at the top of the triangle or, for a different look, sew up both sides of the seam on either side of the zipper. Along the hemline, trim the fabric to match the curve of the skirt. On the wrong side, trim away excess fabric along both sides of the V seam.

8. *Stitch the side seams.* With right sides together, pin the skirt front to the skirt back and try the skirt on to test how it fits. Make any necessary adjustments, then stitch the skirt together at the side seams. Finger-press the seam allowances open and topstitch along both sides of the seam, using a narrow zigzag stitch.

9. *Make a pocket.* Now is the time to embellish the pocket fabric any way you like. Just for fun, we used a grommet setter to add a grommet to the right side of the fabric. For the pocket flap, copy our shape or make up your own. We stitched two rows of topstitching around the edges, using a contrasting thread. If you want to make a buttonhole, do that before you sew the flap to the skirt. When you're ready, center the pocket and flap over a side seam and edgestitch it in place, leaving the top edge open. Other options for fastening the pocket include stitching on Velcro or using a snap setter to add a snap.

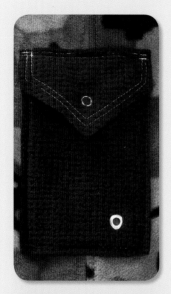

STEP 9

10. *Embellish the waistline.* Pin the twill tape to the right side of the skirt, ¼" to ½" away from the skirt's raw edge. Edgestitch in place. Turn under the raw ends of the twill tape at the zipper seam allowance edge.

11. *Make the ruffle.* With right sides up, overlap the ends of the ruffle strips and stitch them in place with two rows of narrow zigzagging. You can repeat this on the other ends to make one long loop, or leave the ruffle as a strip until after you've stitched it to the bottom of the skirt. Decide which side will be the bottom hem, and machine-stitch a row of straight stitches ½" away from the raw edge.

STEP 11

12. *Stitch the ruffle to the skirt.* You have two choices here for making the ruffle gathers. With either method, the ruffle is sewn to the lower edge of the skirt with both fabrics right sides up and the waffle fleece on top of the camouflage fleece. Once you've sewn the ruffle to the skirt, overlap the ruffle ends and stitch in place with two rows of zigzag stitching (as in step 11).

- You can use the traditional method of making ruffles as described for the peplum section of the Babydoll jacket. (*See pages* 84-85.) This involves making two rows of basting stitches, pinning the ruffle to the skirt at intervals, and pulling on the basting threads to evenly distribute the gathers.

- Or, you can jump in and try our more free-style "scrunching" method to attach the ruffle. (*See photo below*.) The gathers won't be as evenly distributed, but if that doesn't matter to you, it's a less fussy, faster way to go. Try it on some scrap fleece to see if you like it: Put two fabrics together with the ruffle fabric on top. As you stitch, scrunch the upper ruffle fabric by pushing it with your finger against the presser foot. This forces it to bunch up under the needle as the top fabric feeds more quickly than the lower fabric.

STEP 12

GIVE IT A WHIRL!

Snaps or grommets usually come with a special tool for setting them in place. If you decide to go for it, practice first on scraps of fleece until you get the hang of it. Of course, by using twill tape with grommets already in place, you can get the effect without doing the work!

I F CHOCOLATE IS THE PRIMO COMFORT FOOD, fleece has got to be the perfect comfort clothing. Snuggly soft and toasty warm, there's nothing like wrapping up in fleece. Whether you're indoors at home, at the gym, or at a spa, you'll always be dressed to relax.

5

Get Your Fleece On

Beauty and the Fleece

This delicious after-yoga wrap is the perfect alchemy of classic elements, made with velvety paisley fleece and shimmering velour in jeweled tones of aquamarine, topaz, and bronze. Iridescent organza ribbon accents the wrap's neckline and serves to tie the overlapping front sections. Each sleeve is transformed with 16" velour godets.

Stuff You Need

1½ yards of 58"–60" medium-weight fleece

½ yard of 45"–60" lightweight brushed velour fleece or knit fabric

3 yards of ½" sheer organza ribbon

2 buttons, ¾" diameter

Matching or contrasting polyester thread

What You'll Do

Make a body template and cutting guide

Cut the fabric

Stitch and shape the wrap to fit

Make godets and attach the sleeves

Embellish with trim and add ties

Our finished length: 22"

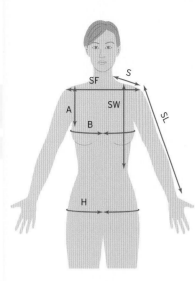

VITAL STATISTICS

To make the yoga wrap, you'll need the following measurements:

S = _____" *Shoulder.* Distance from side of neck to shoulder tip.

SF = _____" *Shoulder front.* The distance from shoulder tip to shoulder tip across the front of your body.

B = _____" *Bust.* The bust measurement around your body.

H = _____" *Hip.* The distance around the fullest part of your hips.

SW = _____" *Shoulder to Waist.* The distance from your shoulder (over the widest part of your bust) to your waist.

SL = _____" *Sleeve length.* Desired length of sleeve from shoulder to wrist.

A = _____" *Armhole depth.* Desired finished depth of the armhole.

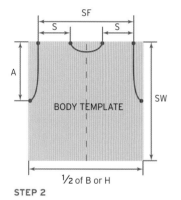

STEP 2

STEP 4 (next page)

MEASURE AND CUT

1. *Take your measurements.* Measure yourself and fill in the blanks under Vital Statistics on this page.

2. *Make a body template.* Draft a body template as instructed below. If you've already made one, just be sure to mark the shoulder to waist measurement and use that length for cutting.

- For the width of the template, use your bust or your hip measurement (whichever is larger) divided by 2.

- For the length, use the SW measurement.

- Draw a line down the center of the template to indicate the center line of the template. Center the SF measurement at the top of the template.

- Plot the S measurements from both sides of the SF measurement.

- Plot the A measurements from each top corner.

- You can draw curved lines for your neck and armhole, but you won't actually shape the fabric until later.

3. *Make a cutting guide — or not!* You will be using this template full size (instead of folded in half), and only need to add ½" for seam allowances on all sides. It's so straightforward, you could use the body template without making a cutting guide, as long as you remember to cut the fabric ½" larger on all sides. Our cutting layout shows what the cutting guide would look like, if you decide to go that route.

4. *Cut out the pieces.* Fold the fleece with right sides together and the greatest stretch running horizontally. Cut three pieces for the body of the wrap — one for the back (on a single layer of fabric) and two for the front (on folded fabric). On all three pieces, mark each shoulder and armhole point with a pin.

5. *Cut out the sleeve blocks.* Also from the fleece, cut two rectangles based on the following:

A = armhole depth ____" x 2 = ____" + 1" for two seam allowances = ____"

B = sleeve length ____" + 1" for two seam allowances = ____"

6. *Cut out the godet for the sleeve.* From the secondary fabric, measure and cut two 18" x 18" squares.

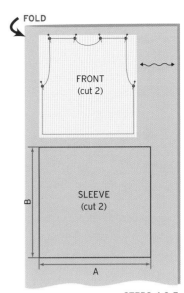

STEPS 4 & 5

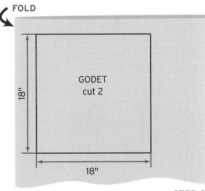

STEP 6

WRAP VARIATION

Cozy Coverup

For a more practical version of this wrap, skip the godets and make close-fitting sleeves. Our blue wrap also has sturdier ties, made with strips of fleece that have been folded in half and zig-zagged down their length.

STEP 7

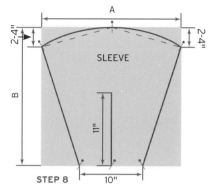

STEP 8

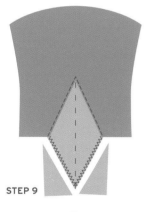

STEP 9

STEP 9

PUT IT TOGETHER

7. *Shape and stitch the body pieces.* For the wraparound effect, cut off one corner on opposite sides of the two front pieces. Make your first cuts conservative, then stitch the front pieces to the back piece, right sides together, at the shoulder seams between the pins. Put the wrap on and decide how much more to trim off. Also, pin the fabric together at the armhole depth and plot the shape of the armholes. Mark these shapes with chalk or pins, then take off the wrap and check that the sides match before you cut.

8. *Shape the sleeves.* Follow the instructions on page 78 for shaping the sleeves. The only difference is a more narrow width at the wrist (ours is 10") and an 11" slash at the center, starting at the lower edge of the sleeve.

9. *Stitch the sleeve godet.* With right sides up, open and pin the slashed sleeve to the godet fabric block. Machine-stitch the V-opening close to the raw edge of the fleece. On the wrong side, trim away excess velour fabric along both sides of the V, and finish the seam allowance with zigzag stitching or pinked edges.

To form a diamond-shape, fold the godet fabric in half and mark the center point at the far edge. Draw diagonal lines from the fleece to the center point on both sides. Cut the fabric, then zigzag close to the raw edge. *Note:* Velour and knit fabrics don't ravel much, so there's no need to turn an edge. If you use a fabric that frays, allow ½"–1" for a hem before you cut the diamond shape.

POWER POINT

The top peak of a godet is just begging for embellishment. Here's where your vintage buttons or other select goodies can provide just the right finishing touch for your one-of-a-kind garment.

10. *Attach the sleeves.* With right sides together, center the sleeves over the shoulder seam and machine-stitch in place.

11. *Stitch the side seams.* With right sides together, pin the sleeves and side seams together. On each side, stitch from cuff to hem, back-tacking at each end.

12. *Finish the wrap.* If desired, turn under the hem edge ½" and stitch close to the raw edge. Pin the organza ribbon around the neck and front opening edges and zigzag in place down the center of the ribbon. Cut four 12" lengths of ribbon for ties and hand-sew them to the waistline and corners of each front piece.

STEP 10

STEP 11

WRAP VARIATION

Geisha Girl

This full length, ivory fleece spa robe is soothing to the touch and meditative to wear. We've taken the yoga warm-up and extended the length to the ankles, adding a 24" embroidered satin godet at each side seam. If you don't care for godets, add width at the center front hemline or a center back slit for walking ease. The sleeves are finished with a 2½" embroidered satin band to match the godets.

Depluske Mode

Perfect for lounging, this bubble-gum pink robe has all the details for comfort: a shawl collar, patch pockets, dainty floral crocheted appliqués and a matching belt. Only the robe pockets and sleeves are hemmed, all other fabric edges are left unfinished. Snuggle up!

Stuff You Need

2½-3 yards of 58"-60" medium-weight fleece

½ yards of ¼" ribbon

2 crocheted flower appliqués

Matching or contrasting polyester thread

What You'll Do

Make a body template and cutting guide

Cut the fabric

Stitch and shape the robe to fit

Shape and attach the sleeves

Stitch the sides

Make a belt and belt loops

Embellish and stitch on pockets

Our finished length: 49"

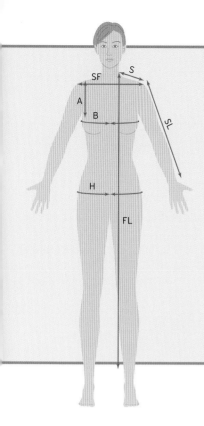

ViTAL STATiSTiCS

To make the robe, you'll need the following measurements:

S = _____" *Shoulder.* Distance from side of neck to shoulder tip.

SF = _____" *Shoulder front.* Distance from shoulder tip to shoulder tip across the front of your body.

B = _____" *Bust.* The bust measurement around your body.

H = _____" *Hip.* The distance around the fullest part of your hips.

FL = _____" *Front length.* Desired length from neck to hem.

SL = _____" *Sleeve length.* Desired length of sleeve from shoulder to wrist.

A = _____" *Armhole depth.* Desired finished depth of the armhole.

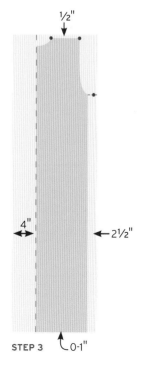

STEP 3

MEASURE AND CUT

1. *Take your measurements.* Measure yourself and fill in the blanks under Vital Statistics on this page.

2. *Make a body template.* Draft a body template as instructed on page 98. The only difference is the length. If you've already made a body template for a jacket or top, you can use it with an adjusted length based on the FL measurement.

3. *Make a cutting guide.* Refer to the pointers on page 77 for making a cutting guide. Adjustments for this project are as follows:

- Top: ½" seam allowance

- Bottom: your choice of allowance for hem (we did not hem ours)

- Left side: 4" for front overlap

- Right side: 2" or more for ease plus ½" for seam allowance

4. Cut out the robe body. Fold the fleece with right sides together and the greatest stretch running horizontally. Cut a block for the back along the fold; the overlap is not needed for the back, so let the cutting guide overlap the folded edge by 4". Cut another block through two layers for the front pieces. On all three pieces, mark each shoulder and armhole point with a pin.

5. Cut out the two sleeve blocks. Cut two rectangles based on the following:

A = armhole depth ____" x 2 = ____"
     + 1" for two seam allowances = ____"

B = sleeve length ____" + ½" seam allowances at top
     + 2" for cuff hem = ____"

6. Cut out the remaining pieces.

● For the belt: cut a 4" x 30" rectangle, positioned on the fold

● For the collar: cut a 6" x 30" rectangle, positioned on the fold

● For the pockets: measure a 6" x 8" rectangle and cut two

● For belt loops: measure a ¾" x 3" rectangle and cut two

PUT IT TOGETHER

7. Stitch the shoulders. With right sides together, machine-stitch the front pieces to the back piece at the shoulder seams between the pins. Mark the armhole depth with a pin or marker.

8. Shape the robe. Turn the robe right sides out and put it on. Check the width and angle of the shoulder seam, the depth of the armhole, the length, and the amount of overlap in front. Make adjustments as needed. Using the armhole-depth marker as a guide, turn under the fabric at the armhole edges and pin, or mark with chalk where you want to cut. Do the same to make a V at the neckline. Take off the robe and check that the sides match before cutting the neck and armhole shapes.

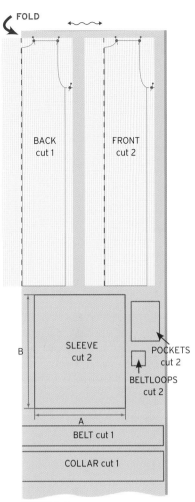

STEPS 4-6

STEP 7

STEP 8

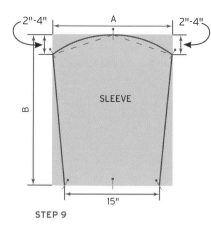

2"-4" | A | 2"-4"

B

SLEEVE

15"

STEP 9

9. Shape the sleeves. Follow the instructions on page 78 for shaping the sleeves. The only difference is to add more width at the wrist for comfort (ours is 15").

10. Attach the sleeves. With right sides together, center the sleeves over the shoulder seam and machine-stitch in place.

11. Stitch the side seams and hem. With right sides together, pin the jacket sleeves and side seams together. On each side of the robe, stitch from cuff to hemline, backtacking at each end. Turn under each sleeve hem 2" and stitch in place. At the robe bottom hem and front, zigzag along the raw edges.

12. Stitch the collar. Turn the robe inside out and pin the *right* side of the collar to the *wrong* side of the robe. Center the band at the back of the neck so the ends of the collars with line up with each other on the sides. Stitch the collar to the robe and trim the seam allowance to ¼". Try on the robe and turn back the collar. With pins or chalk, mark the shape you want for the shawl collar. Check that the sides match before you trim away fabric.

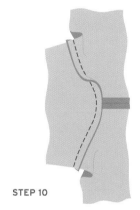

STEP 10

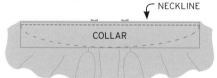

NECKLINE

COLLAR

STEP 12

STEP 11

13. Stitch the belt and belt loops. With right sides out, fold the belt in half lengthwise and machine-stitch on three sides. (Since fleece doesn't fray, there's no need to turn the fleece inside out, as you would if making a belt from a woven fabric.) This makes a 2" wide belt. Try on the robe and mark where you want your belt loops to be sewn at the side seams. Machine-stitch the belt loops to the right side of the robe side seam.

14. *Stitch the pockets.* Fold under 2" along the top edge of the pocket fabric piece. Machine-stitch a 6" length of ribbon across the pocket edge, catching the folded edge underneath. Machine-stitch a crocheted flower appliqué to the center of each ribbon. Machine-stitch the pockets to the robe fronts near the waistline.

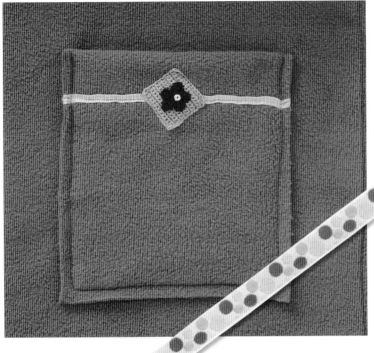

ROBE VARIATION

Kozy Kid Kimono

With your child's measurements and a few minor adjustments (smaller pockets, shorter collar and belt pieces), you can easily make a pint-sized plush version of this robe. Look for playful prints and add your own kid-friendly embellishments.

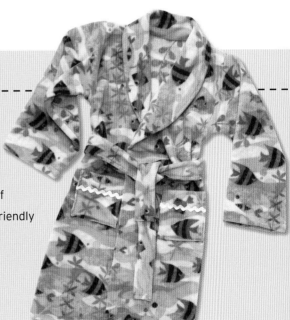

Fleece Navidad

What better way to relax than wearing toasty fleece pajama bottoms? The drawstring waistline and wide roomy legs are easily made to fit yourself, family, or friends — male or female, kids included! Once you get the hang of drafting the pattern, you can turn out a pair of pants in about an hour. You don't need to worry about being 100 percent exact. The natural stretchiness of fleece can accommodate "close enough."

Stuff You Need

1½ to 2 yards of 58"-60" print fleece

1 to 1½ yards of ½"-⅝" ribbon for the drawstring

Matching or contrasting polyester thread

What You'll Do

Make a body template and cutting guide

Cut out the pieces

Stitch the seams

Make a casing and insert the drawstring

Hem the cuffs

Our finished length: 39"

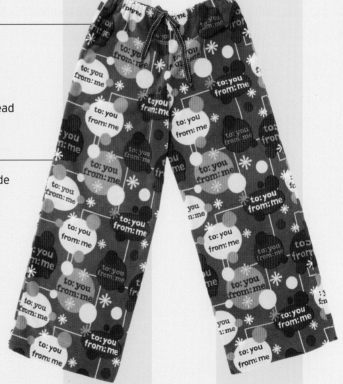

VITAL STATISTICS

To make these pants and others in this chapter, you'll need the following measurements:

W = _____" *Waist.* The distance around your body at the waistline (or just below the waist, if preferred)

H = _____" *Hips.* The distance around the fullest part of your hips.

S = _____" *Seat.* When seated on a flat chair or table, the distance from your natural waistline to the chair or table.

L = _____" *Finished length.* The finished desired length from waistline to hem.

BW = _____" *Bottom width.* The desired finished width of the bottom hem.

MEASURE AND CUT

1. *Take your measurements.* Measure yourself and fill in the blanks under Vital Statistics on this page.

2. *Do the math.* Use the measurements in Vital Statistics to fill in the blanks below. *Note:* since the pants will pull on over your hips and be gathered by a drawstring, the hip measurement is used for the waistline. (You'll need the waistline measurement for the next project.)

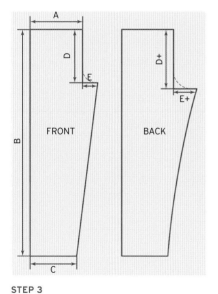

A = H (hips) _____" ÷ 4 = _____"

B = L (length) _____"

C = BW (bottom width) _____" ÷ 2 = _____"

D = S (seat) _____"

E = crotch margin: 1½" to 2½" (or more if you're a large size)
  = _____"

For the back, you will make an adjustment to allow for your backside. (If you are very slim, the front and back pieces can be pretty much the same.)

D+ = S (seat) _____" + 1" to 2" = _____"

E+ = crotch margin: 2" to 4" (or more if you're a large size)
  = _____"

STEP 3

3. Make a body template. Lay out a large sheet of paper and plot your measurements, one line at a time.

For the front: start with line A, then draw lines B through E. It helps to go in order. Draw a curved line at the corner of D and E, then connect E to C to complete the pattern.

For the back: draw lines A through C as before, then use the D+ and E+ measurements. Once again, draw a curved line at the corner of D and E, then connect E to C to complete the pattern. Curve the line as shown rather than making a perfectly straight line.

Label your pieces Front and Back to keep track, and cut them out.

4. Make a cutting guide. On separate sheets of paper, trace each template and adjust the margins as follows:

- Top: add 1½" for the drawstring casing

- Inside leg: add ½" for seam allowance

- Outside leg: add 1½" for ease and ½" for seam allowance

- Bottom: your choice of allowance for hem (we added 3")

5. Cut out the pieces. Fold the fleece with right sides together and the greatest stretch running horizontally. It's easier to cut the fabric on the grain if you line up the straight side of each template with the sides of the folded fleece. To conserve fabric, turn over the front template and line it up with the selvage.

ON THE GRID

When drawing a template, it's important to keep your lines straight and the corners at right angles. One really cool way to do this is to plot your templates on the back of gift wrap paper with a 1" grid. (If you do find one with a grid, don't assume that the squares are 1" — measure them.) Otherwise, you can use a right-angle triangle or a book to keep your corners square.

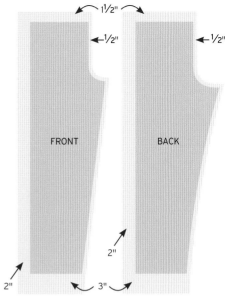

STEP 4

STEP 5

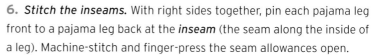

PUT IT TOGETHER

6. *Stitch the inseams.* With right sides together, pin each pajama leg front to a pajama leg back at the **inseam** (the seam along the inside of a leg). Machine-stitch and finger-press the seam allowances open.

7. *Stitch the crotch seam.* With right sides together, pin the pajama fronts and backs together and machine-stitch the crotch seam. Finger-press the seam allowances open.

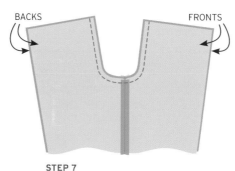

STEP 6   STEP 7   STEP 8

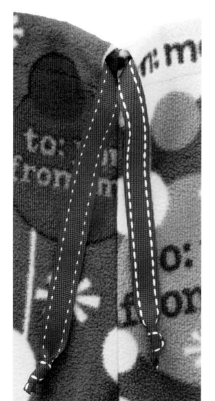

8. *Stitch the side seams.* With right sides together, pin the pants front and back together at the side seams and machine-stitch. Finger-press the seam allowances open.

9. *Make the drawstring casing.* With the pants wrong side out, fold 1½" of fleece to the inside at the waistline and stitch 1" from the edge. Turn the pants right side out and open up the center seam in the front just enough to thread the drawstring through the casing.

10. *Stitch the cuffs.* Turn 3" of fleece to the inside and stitch two straight lines along the edge, about ¼" apart. This adds a bit of weight to the bottom of the pants and gives the appearance of a cuff.

PAJAMA VARIATION

Twinkle, Twinkle

You'll want to stay in bed all day in this plush velour fleece. These pajama pants are made the same way as Fleece Navidad, except for three things outlined below:

1. Contrasting fabric and trim at the bottom of the legs.

   a. Trace the bottom 6" of your pants leg and use it as a guide to cut 4 bands of contrasting fabric. When you cut the pants, make them 6" shorter at the bottom.

   b. With right sides together, pin each band to the bottom of each leg and stitch a ½" seam.

   c. Finger-press both seam allowances toward the hemline, then cover each seam with mini rickrack and stitch. When all four cuffs are done, sew the pants together.

2. An elastic waistline instead of a drawstring.

   a. Make the casing as instructed, but leave an opening to insert the elastic.

   b. Cut a length of ¾" elastic to fit comfortably around your waist. Insert the elastic into the casing and machine-stitch the ends of the elastic together. Machine-stitch the casing opening closed.

3. No cuff at the ankle. This version simply has 1½" of fabric turned under and stitched with a narrow zigzag.

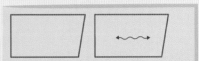

STEP 1a

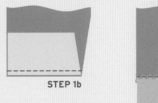

STEP 1b　　　　**STEP 1c**

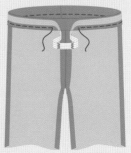

STEP 2b

Toasty Buns

These carefree, waffle fleece pants are so comfortable to wear, you'll feel enlightened just wearing them. The wide stretchy waistband is designed to be worn just below the waist — the secret to a great fit without too much bulk at the top. The trim around the legs is a snap to make from scraps of fleece in any color you like.

Stuff You Need

1½ to 2 yards of 58"-60" solid color waffle fleece

¼ yard or less of a contrasting color of fleece

Matching or contrasting polyester thread

What You'll Do

Make a body template and cutting guide

Cut out the pieces

Stitch the seams

Make and attach a waistband

Embellish the legs

Hem the cuffs

Our finished length: 33"

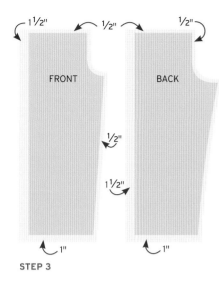

FRONT

1½" ½" ½"

BACK

½"

1½"

1" 1"

STEP 3

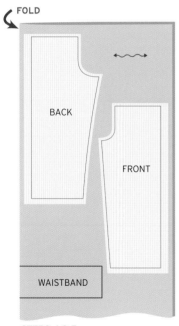

FOLD

BACK

FRONT

WAISTBAND

STEPS 4 & 5

MEASURE AND CUT

1. *Take your measurements.* Measure yourself and fill in the blanks under Vital Statistics on page 110.

2. *Make a body template.* Follow the instructions on page 110 for making a body template, with these differences:

- These pants are designed to be wider at the bottom, so add 2" to 3" to the BW measurement as desired.

- You will be adding a 3" wide waistband that is 2½" wide when attached. Go ahead and make the template as usual, then cut or fold 2½" off the top.

3. *Make a cutting guide.* On separate sheets of paper, trace each template and adjust the margins as follows:

- Top: having allowed for the 2½" waistband, add ½" for seam allowance

- Inside leg: add ½" for seam allowance

- Outside leg: add 1" for ease and ½" for seam allowance

- Bottom: your choice of allowance for hem (we added 1")

4. *Cut out the pants.* Fold the fleece with right sides together and the greatest stretch running across (so the pants will have more stretch side to side). It's easier to cut the fabric on the grain if you line up the straight side of each template with the sides of the folded fleece. To conserve fabric, turn over the front template and line it up with the selvage.

5. *Cut out the waistband.* You need a rectangle that is 6" wide. The length should be your waistline measurement plus 1" for ease and 1" for seam allowances. Divide that number in half and cut the waistband on the fold.

6. *Cut out the embellishments.* From a contrasting scrap of fleece, cut two ½" strips the length of your BW measurement + 8"–10".

PUT IT TOGETHER

7. *Stitch the inseams.* With right sides together, pin each pant leg front to a pant leg back at the *inseam* (the seam along the inside of a leg). If desired, finger-press the seam allowance toward the pants back and topstitch through all layers ¼" away from the seam. (*See example on page* 25.)

BACK

FRONT

STEP 7

8. *Stitch the crotch seam.* With right sides together, pin the fronts and backs together and machine-stitch the crotch seam. If desired, finger-press the seam allowance to one side and topstitch through all layers ¼" away from the seam.

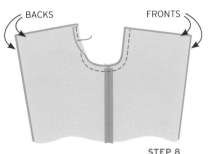

BACKS FRONTS

STEP 8

9. *Stitch the side seams.* With right sides together, pin the pants front and back together at the side seams and machine-stitch. If desired, finger-press the seam allowance toward the pants back and topstitch through all layers ¼" away from the seam.

10. *Stitch the waistband.* With right sides together, stitch the waistband center back seam with a narrow zigzag stitch. Finger-press the seam allowance open. With wrong sides together, fold the waistband in half lengthwise. With right sides together, pin the lower open edge of the waistband to the upper edge of the pants, matching center backs, and stretching waistband to fit as needed. Machine-stitch and finger-press the seam allowance toward pants. Topstitch through all layers ¼" from the seam.

STEP 9

11. *Hem and embellish.* Turn under a 1" hem on each pants leg and machine-stitch with two parallel rows of stitching. For each leg, embellish by stitching the ½" wide strip of contrasting fleece fabric to the pants legs, 6" from the hem. Trim off the extra, tie it into a bow, and machine-stitch in place.

STEP 10

$\mathcal{L}$ITTLE ONES LOVE FLEECE TOO. What better way to pamper your favorite little darlings? Just wait until you see them wrapped up in these soft, cozy projects. Easy-care, machine-washable fleece is a bonus for moms, too.

Baby Got Fleece

Snuggle Time

This supersoft blanket is sure to become baby's favorite "blankie." Just stitch together rectangles of your favorite fleece fabric, then embellish it with irresistible trims and appliqués. You can stitch the fleece with the raw edges out or raw edges in since fraying is never an issue when handling and washing fleece.

Stuff You Need

1⅛ yards of 58"-60" ribbed medium-weight fleece

2¾ yards of 1¼" floral lace trim

11 daisy floral appliqués, ⅞" diameter

Matching or contrasting polyester thread

What You'll Do

Cut out the blanket

Stitch the sides and turn inside out

Topstitch and embellish

Our finished size: 28" x 38"

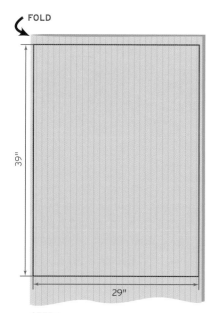

FOLD

39"

29"

STEP 1

STEP 2

MAKE IT!

1. *Measure and cut.* Fold the fleece with right sides together and lay it out smooth on a cutting surface. With a rotary cutter and mat (*see page* 10), cut out two 29" x 39" rectangles.

2. *Stitch the sides.* Pin the blanket pieces with right sides together. Stitch around the blanket using a ½" seam allowance and leave a 4" opening for turning.

3. *Topstitch the sides.* Turn the blanket right sides out. Topstitch about ¼"–⅜" away from the edge, all around the blanket.

4. *Embellish.* Pin the floral trim to one side of the blanket, 1" away from edges. Miter the trim at each corner, as described on the opposite page. Stitch the trim in place. Position the daisy appliqués on the blanket – in a pattern or randomly – and machine-stitch or hand-sew them in place through all layers of fabric.

Turning a Neat Corner

When sewing ribbon or trim around a corner, mitering (forming a right angle with a 45-degree cut or fold) is very tidy way to go. The look resembles the corners of a picture frame – a classic way to finish off embellished blanket corners. Here's how you do it:

1. On one side of the blanket, edgestitch the ribbon to the corner along the ribbon's outside edge.

2. Fold the ribbon back, then refold it at a 45-degree angle. You don't have to stitch the folded section underneath, but if you're working with a wide ribbon, stitching will help to hold it in place. Test the angle first, though, to make sure the ribbon will lay flat in step 3.

3. Pin the refolded ribbon and continue to edgestitch the ribbon in place. After stitching around the whole blanket, run another line of stitches on the opposite side of the ribbon.

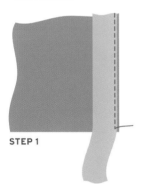

STEP 1   STEP 2   STEP 3

FLEECE SHORTCUT

For a super-speedy baby blanket, cut long 2"-3" wide strips of fleece and attach them to the sides of a central rectangle using a wide zigzag stitch. Trim the outermost edges with pinking shears.

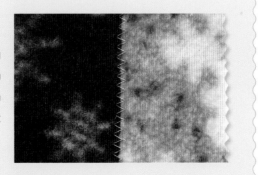

Fleece Tight

Baby's in the hood! Pamper your little one at bathtime with this sky blue polka-dot hooded blanket. You can fringe the blanket edges and add a tassel at the top. For playful hood edging variations, try laces, ribbons, trims, or bias bindings.

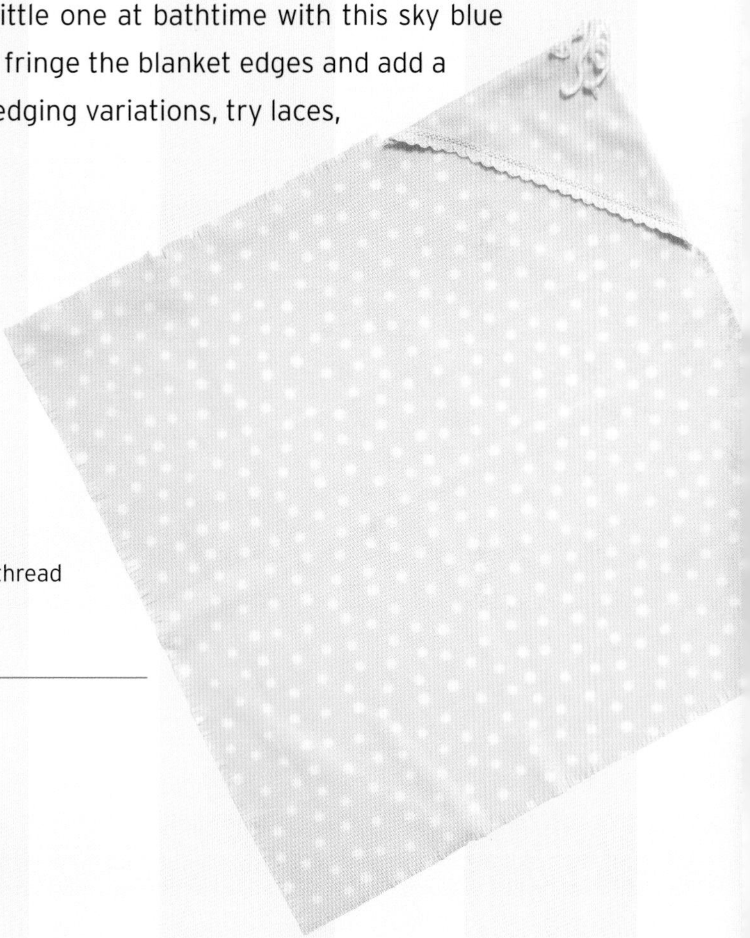

Stuff You Need

1 yard of 58"–60" polka-dot medium-weight fleece

⅛ yard of solid-color medium-weight fleece

½ yard of trim or ribbon

Matching or contrasting polyester thread

What You'll Do

Cut out the blanket pieces

Make the tassel

Embellish and stitch the hood

Make the fringe

Our finished size: 33" x 33"

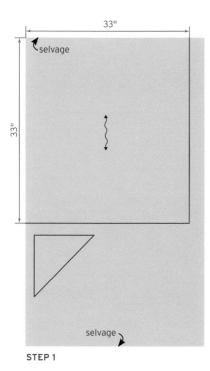

STEP 1

STEP 2

MAKE IT!

1. *Cut it out.* You can make the blanket whatever size you like as long as you maintain the shape as a square. This will keep the folded sides of the blanket symmetrical (the same size) once you place the hood on one corner. Lay the fleece out smooth on a cutting surface and cut the square (ours is 33" x 33"). (*See page* 19.) If you prefer, fold the fleece in half and cut the square on the fold (16½" x 33").

For the hood: Draw a 12" square, then draw a line diagonally across (from opposite corners) to form a triangle. Cut one.

For the tassels: Cut the tassels from the same fleece or a from a fleece in a complementary color (we used white). You will need two ½" x 12" strips cut along the fabric's crosswise grain (the direction with the greatest stretch).

2. *Make the tassels.* Making tassels is a great way to take advantage of fleece's natural ability to curl. Take each of the ½" x 12" strips and pull the ends apart as far as they will go. This causes the fleece to roll up like a cord and curl softly. (*See page* 16.) If your strip breaks when you pull on it, cut another strip that is a little wider. Strips that are ¼" to ½" in width usually work best with this technique, and the result will vary depending on the type and weight of fleece that you use. Put the two tassel strips together and fold them to make a four-strand tassel. Pin the ends together and set it aside for now.

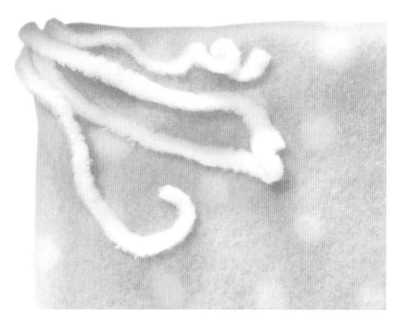

3. *Embellish the hood.* On the right side of the fabric, stitch the trim to the hood triangle along its longest (diagonal) edge.

4. *Stitch the hood corner.* Pin the folded corner of the tassel to one corner of the blanket (on the right side of the fabric), with the tassel laying on the blanket. With right sides together, pin the hood triangle to the same corner. The tassel will be covered by the hood, with only the folded ends sticking out at the corner. Edgestitch the hood to the blanket, stitching through all layers. Turn the hood right sides out and fluff up the tassel.

← tip of tassel

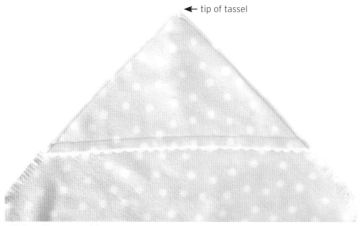

stitch on the wrong side

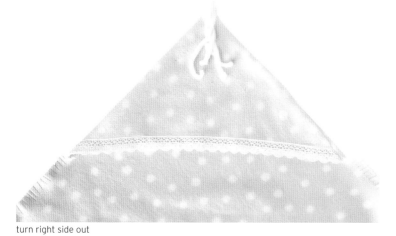

turn right side out

FASTER FRINGE

Here's a tip for making evenly cut fringe that is all the same length. Place your fleece between two books, and allow the fabric to hang over by ½" (or the length you want the fringe to be). As you cut the fringe with scissors, the books will stop the scissors in the same place each time.

5. *Create the fringe.* To make fringe around the blanket edges, cut the fleece into narrow strips approximately 1" long and ³⁄₈" wide, stopping at the edges of the triangle hood.

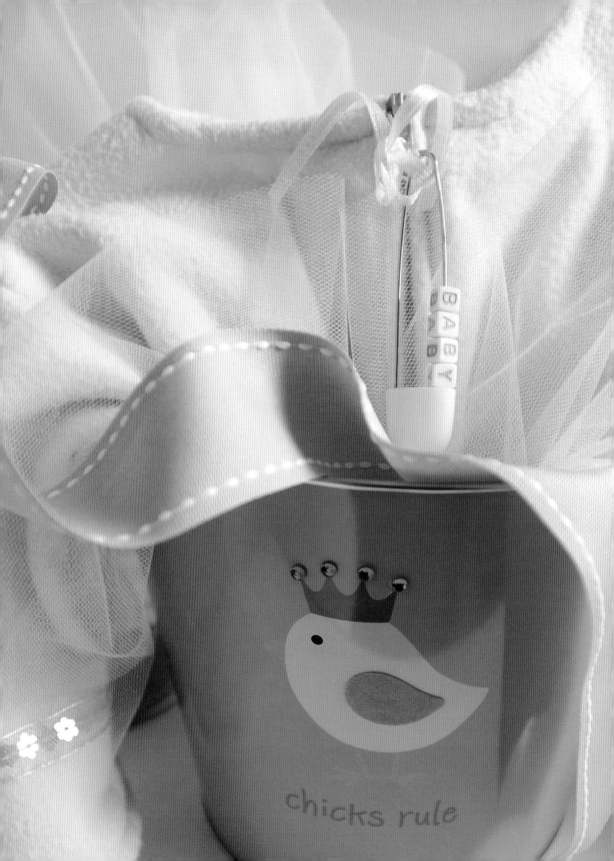

Bundle of Joy

Few things say "bundle of joy" as easily as a baby bunting. Chicks dig it, and so will baby boys! Surround your favorite baby with love, warmth, and comfort in this zip-up-the-front fleece bunting. It can be made with micro-fleece or heavier fleece, as you like.

Stuff You Need

1 yard of 58"–60" medium-weight plush fleece

2 yards of ½" decorative ribbon or trim

1 matching 20" zipper

Matching or contrasting polyester thread

What You'll Do

Make a pattern

Cut out the pieces

Put in the zipper

Embellish

Stitch the sleeves and bunting

Finish the neckline edge

Our finished size: 18" x 25"

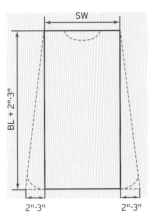

STEP 2

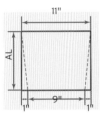

STEP 2

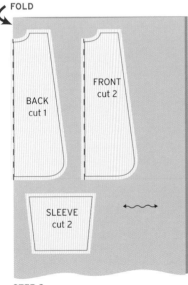

STEP 3

MEASURE AND CUT

1. *Take measurements.* You only need three measurements to get started. For a custom fit, go by the actual baby rather than any size chart you might find. Fill in the blanks below:

SW = ____" *Shoulder width.* The distance from shoulder to shoulder.

BL = ____" *Body length.* The distance from neck to toes (with outstretched legs).

AL = ____" *Arm length.* The distance from shoulder to wrist (with outstretched arm).

2. *Make a pattern.* Draw a rectangle using SW for the width and the BL + 2" to 3" for the length. Technically, you could use this rectangle "as is" to make the bunting. However, for a more elegant shape and extra kicking room, extend the width of the bottom line by 2" to 3" on either side. Draw a line from the shoulder width to the new bottom width on both sides and round off the bottom corners. Cut out a shallow curve for the neckline.

For the sleeves: Draw a rectangle that is 11" across (this is the shoulder line), and use the AL measurement for the sides. Measure in 1" on either side of the bottom line (this is the cuff), leaving a width of 9". Draw new side lines from shoulder to cuff.

3. *Cut out the pieces.* Fold the fleece with right sides together and the greatest stretch running horizontally. Fold the bunting pattern in half and add ½" on all sides for seam allowance. Cut out one back piece on the fold, leaving out the middle seam allowance. Cut out two fronts and two sleeves.

PUT IT TOGETHER

4. *Put in the zipper.* With right sides together, baste the front pieces together at the center seam. Open up the front pieces and finger-press the seam open. On the wrong side of the fabric, center the zipper face-down on the seam. Allow the top of the zipper cloth (not the teeth) to barely overlap the neckline edge. Baste the zipper onto the seam (or use basting tape), then topstitch in place. *(See page 30.)*

5. *Embellish the bunting.* Pin the trim to the right sides of both sleeves about 3" from the cuff edges. Likewise, pin the trim to the front and back pieces about 3" from the hem edges. Stitch the trim in place.

6. *Stitch the shoulder seams.* With right sides together, stitch the front of the bunting to the back at the shoulders. Finger-press the seam allowances open.

7. *Stitch the sleeves.* Turn under the raw edges of each cuff by ½" and topstitch in place. Fold each sleeve in half and mark the center of the shoulder edge with a pin. With right sides together, line up that spot with the shoulder seams of the bunting. Pin the sleeve in place, then stitch.

STEP 4

STEP 5

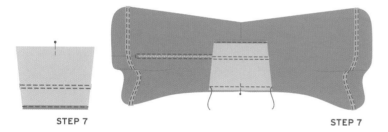

STEP 7   STEP 7

8. *Stitch the side seams.* With right sides together, stitch the bunting front to the bunting back, stitching from sleeve hem to sleeve hem. Turn right sides out.

9. *Finish the neck opening.* Turn under the neck opening by ½" and topstitch in place. Tie an embellishment to the zipper top if desired. *Note:* The pin you see on page 128 is NOT a real pin; it will not open. Make sure that the embellishment you use is safe for the baby.

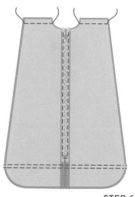

STEP 6

Pixie Fleece

Flowers, ribbons, bows, and bells add up to a whimsical combination for baby's first hat and booties set. Use your imagination to enter a world as whimsical as Neverland. The design possibilities are endless.

Stuff You Need

½ yard of 58"-60" fleece

1 yard of ½" floral embroidered ribbon

1½ yard of ⅝" crushed velvet ribbon

½ yard of ½" sheer organza ribbon

3 bells, ½" in diameter

Matching or contrasting polyester thread

Fleece fabric scraps

What You'll Do

Take measurements

Make the patterns

Cut out the pieces

Embellish and stitch

Our finished hat length: 13"

Our finished booties length: 3½"

MEASURE AND CUT

1. *Take measurements.* Fill in the blanks below:

HC = _____" *Head circumference.* The distance around the baby's head, just above the ears.

F = _____" *Foot.* Length of the foot from heel to toe.

2. *Make the patterns.* On a piece of paper, do the following.

For the hat: Draw a 15"-tall triangle with a base that is the HC measurement ÷ 2 = _____" + 1" for two seam allowances = _____".

For the booties: Trace the template on this page and enlarge it on a photocopier as needed. The length from the heel to the furthest edge of the curled toe should measure F + 1" (½" seam allowance and ½" wiggle room) = _____"

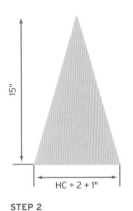

15"

HC ÷ 2 + 1"

STEP 2

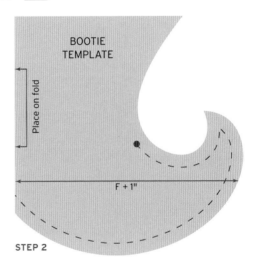

BOOTIE
TEMPLATE

Place on fold

F + 1"

STEP 2

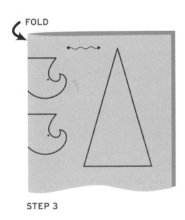

FOLD

STEP 3

3. *Cut out the pieces.* Fold a section of fleece with right sides together and the greatest stretch running horizontally. Place the bootie pattern on the fold and cut two pieces. With a chalk marker or pin, mark the placement of the fabric dot on the wrong side of the bootie fabric pieces. Cut out two pieces for the hat.

MAKE THE HAT

4. *Embellish the hat.* Cut 16 to 20 flowers from the embroidered ribbon and stitch the flowers to the right side of the hat fabric pieces. Don't worry about preserving the shape of each flower — this is more about adding bits of color.

5. *Stitch the seams.* With right sides together, stitch the hat pieces together along both triangle sides. Leave a small opening at the top for inserting the ribbon tassel. Turn the hat right sides out and turn under a ¾" hem at the opening. Machine-stitch in place using a narrow zigzag stitch.

6. *Finish the hat.* Cut three 6" strips of organza ribbon and two 6" strips of velvet ribbon. Stuff the ends into the tip of the hat and hand-sew them in place. Sew a bell to the top of the hat.

INSIDE OUT

With the Babycakes hat and the booties, both right and wrong sides of the fleece will be showing in the finished project. Since most fleece looks the same on both sides, you probably won't notice much of a difference. The instructions, however, refer to the right and wrong sides as a way of helping you keep track of which way to turn the fleece as you sew it.

HAT VARIATION

Babycakes

This sweet alternative hat is a miniature version of the Cupcake hat. Here are some pointers for making this hat:

- Measure the baby's head as you would measure your own. (*See page* 50.) Use those measurements for cutting out the fabric, with one exception: add 4" for the cuff allowance instead of 8".

- Follow the same steps on page 53 for stitching the sides and shaping the top of the hat.

- Before you stitch the last seam on the crown, make a couple of loops with the flower trim and tuck the ends inside the tip of the crown. Stitch in place.

- While the hat is still inside out, turn under the cuff by about 2" and stitch the trim about 1" from the folded edge.

- Turn the hat right side out, then fold up the cuff.

MAKE THE BOOTIES

7. *Embellish the booties.* For each bootie: Lay the fabric out flat with the wrong side facing up. Machine-stitch the floral embroidered ribbon ¾" away from the cuff's straight edge. Turn the bootie over, with the right side facing up. Cut a piece of velvet ribbon 21" long. Machine-tack the center of the ribbon to the center back of the bootie, placing the ribbon 2" from the cuff's straight edge.

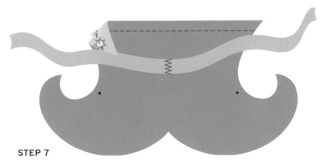

STEP 7

8. *Stitch the booties.* Fold each bootie in half with right sides together and stitch from the folded edge to the dot. Backstitch at both ends to reinforce. Trim the seam allowance close to stitching at toe area.

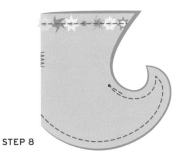

STEP 8

9. *Finish the booties.* Turn the booties right sides out and stuff fleece fabric scraps into the toe seam for shaping and fullness. Hand-sew a bell at the toe point. Turn under the bootie cuffs and tie the velvet ribbon into a bow.

BOOTIE VARIATION

Elfin Magic

Baby's first moccasins are fast and easy to make using our pattern template.

- Before stitching the seams, adorn the cuff with embroidered-hearts ribbon and ³/₄" faux suede fringe. As an alternative to suede fringe, simply fringe the fleece with scissors as described on page 28, making the fringe ½" long and ¼" wide.

- Tack a 22" length of suede cording at the center back of the moccasin. Or, make your own ties with strips of fleece that are ¼" to ³/₈" wide. Pull on the strips until they roll into soft cording. (*See page* 16.)

FOR THE ULTIMATE PAMPERED PET, dress your "best friend" in fleece! Everyone loves the comforting softness of fleece, and your dog is no exception. No-ravel fleece can hold its own with even the friskiest pet, and it's easy to wash and maintain, too.

7

the Fleece Out?

Love 'Dana

Your darling pooch will charm everyone he meets when he's wearing this custom bandana. Add trims and lettering that announce to the world just how you feel about your pet. If you use a print fleece without embellishment, you can make this no-sew project in minutes. Make several for your own dog or as gifts for your favorite neighborhood pups.

Stuff You Need

3/8 yard of 58"–60" medium-weight fleece

3/4 yard orange velvet rickrack

3/4 yard green velvet rickrack

Optional: sew-on decorative letter charms

Matching or contrasting polyester thread

What You'll Do

Make a pattern

Cut out the pieces

Embellish the bandana

Option: Stitch to reinforce the ties

Our finished size: 19" across (not counting ties) x 10" wide

MAKE IT

1. *Measure your dog.* Our bandana triangle is 19" across the top and 10" wide at the point, but you can make a larger or smaller triangle for the bandana based on the size of your dog.

- For the longest side of the triangle (A), go by the distance around your dog's neck. A = _____"

- For the width (B), decide how far down you want the triangle to hang, perhaps the length of the dog's chest. B = _____"

2. *Make the pattern.* The bandana is a triangle-shaped piece of fleece with two narrow fabric extensions for the ties. The simplest approach is to cut the ties as part of the triangle rather than stitching them on as separate pieces. However, do whatever works best for you.

- To draw the bandana pattern (on paper or directly on the fabric), measure the bandana shape as shown. To draw the triangle shape, mark the halfway point of the bandana from the top of the fleece to the bottom width. Draw lines from that point to the bandana sides at the top.

- Our ties are 10" long and ½" deep on both sides, but feel free to experiment. (*See box below.*)

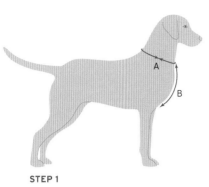

STEP 1

TiED UP iN KNOTS

If your dog is rambunctious, you might want to make stronger ties. Cut them out twice as wide (1" instead of ½"), fold them over, and stitch from end to end across the bandana. If you don't like fleece ties, there's plenty of room to be creative. Invent your own design by adding ties made from twill tape, strips of woven fabric, or anything else that catches your fancy. For a stronger bandana that doesn't stretch out of shape, stitch your tie of choice across the entire upper edge of the bandana triangle.

3. *Cut it out.* Lay the fleece out flat with either side (right or wrong) facing up. The important thing is to have the greatest stretch running horizontally. Be sure to cut out the longest side of the bandana (with the ties) along the crosswise grain.

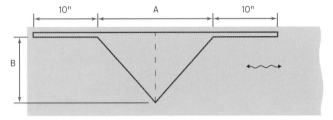

STEP 3

4. *Adjust the ties.* Take advantage of fleece's natural ability to curl into soft cording. Grab the ends of each of the 10" x ½" ties and tug on them until the fleece curls. Fleece strips that are ¼" to ½" in width usually work best with this technique. For added strength, tie a knot at the end of each tie.

5. *Embellish.* To copy our design, stitch a row of green rickrack ½" away from the bandana's hem edges. Stitch a second row of orange rickrack ½" away from the first row. Hand-sew letter charms down the center front of the bandana to spell out L O V E — or perhaps your dog's name.

BANDANA VARIATION

Sports Fan

Support your favorite sports team with pride, with a custom doggy bandana. Clip the edges with pinking shears, and you're done!

Can You See Me Now?

Do you and your four-footed friend enjoy long walks in the great outdoors? For protection and style, outfit your dog in blaze orange – the universal safety color. With this blanket-style doggy vest, the two of you will stand out wherever you go!

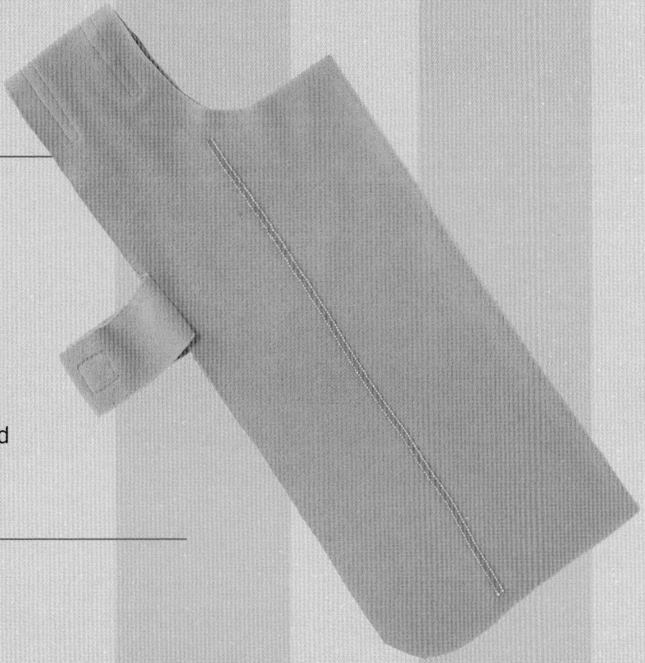

Stuff You Need

⅜ yard of 58"-60" medium-weight fleece for a small dog or up to 1 yard for a large dog

1-2 yards of ribbon, trim, or reflective tape (optional)

4" strip of 1¼" wide sew-on Velcro

Matching or contrasting polyester thread

What You'll Do

Make and test a pattern

Cut out the vest

Stitch on Velcro strips

Embellish

Our finished size: 10" x 16"

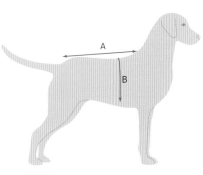

STEP 1

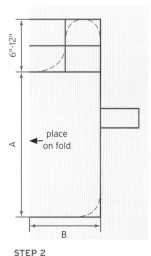

6"-12"

A

← place
on fold

B

STEP 2

MAKE IT

1. *Measure your dog.* You'll need two measurements to make the doggy vest:

- For the finished length of the vest (A), measure your dog from the back of its head to the beginning of its tail. A = ____"

- For the finished width of the vest (B), measure the distance from your dog's backbone to where you want the finished hem to end (pretty much level with the dog's belly). B = ____"

2. *Make the pattern.* To make the pattern, draw directly on the fabric (folded in half) or on a large sheet of paper, as follows:

- Along the fold, draw a rectangle with the length equal to A and the depth equal to B.

- To plot the chest strap, extend the length of the rectangle about 6" (for small dogs) to 12" (for larger dogs), then divide this section into quarters. Don't worry about getting this part exactly right. These fold-over flaps are designed to adjust to the size of your dog.

- Draw two smooth curves and one half circle in the rectangles as shown. Also draw a curve at the opposite corner (the back of the vest).

- Near the center of the bottom edge, draw a belly strap that is 3" wide by about 6". The position of this second adjustable strap is purely guesswork, and you won't know for sure if it's in the best place until you test the pattern on your dog.

3. *Do a test run (optional).* You might want to test the pattern by cutting it from some scrap material before you cut into your fleece fabric. Try the test vest on your dog and check the following items. Make any necessary changes to the pattern.

- Do the length and width fit well?

- Do the chest straps need to be longer or shorter?

- Are the belly straps a good length and in the right place?

- Does the neck curve need to be adjusted?

4. Cut it out. Fold the fleece with right sides together and the greatest stretch running horizontally. Place the vest pattern with the top (the side that will be on the dog's back) on the fold. Cut out the vest as one big piece.

5. Add the Velcro. Put the vest on your dog. Mark a chalk line on the chest straps and belly straps where you want the Velcro strips to be. Take the vest off the dog and stitch the Velcro in place. (*See page* 151.)

6. Embellish. Stitch a strip of trim, ribbon, or reflective tape down the length of the vest, add a zigzag stitch around the borders, or anything else that strikes your fancy.

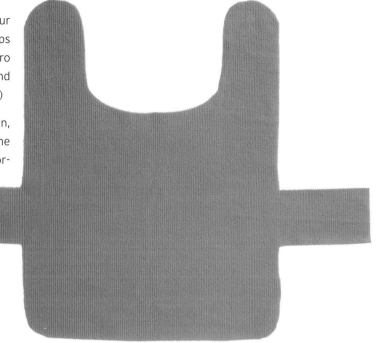

DOGGIE-VEST VARIATION

City Babe

If you're more likely to walk your dog around town than in the woods, the doggy vest is easy to adapt to any style. What a cutie!

Let It Fleece

Though the weather outside is frightful, this double-thickness fleece vest will keep your dog warm and looking mah-velous. Straps adjust for a perfect fit and the side pockets are handy for toting treats. Make it in any color-and-trim combination to suit your pet's personality.

Stuff You Need

¾ yard of 58"-60" medium weight fleece for a small dog or 1½ yards for a large dog

¼ yard of 58"-60" waffle fleece in a contrasting color

1-1½ yards of ¾" twill tape with grommets

4" strip of 1¼" wide sew-on Velcro

½ yard of ⅝" wide sew-on Velcro

Matching or contrasting polyester thread

What You'll Do

Make and test a pattern

Cut out the jacket

Stitch on Velcro strips

Embellish

Our finished length: 12" for a large dog

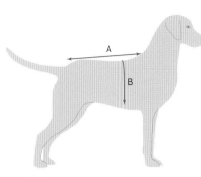

STEP 1

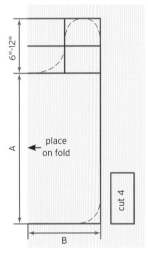

6"–12"

A

place
on fold

cut 4

B

STEP 2

MAKE IT

1. *Measure your dog.* Most of the instructions for this vest are the same as for the vest on page 144, but there are some differences. We will walk you through them, start to finish:

- For the finished length (A), measure your dog from the back of its head to the beginning of its tail. A = _____"

- For the finished width (B), measure the distance from your dog's backbone to where you want the finished hem to end (pretty much level with the dog's belly). B = _____"

2. *Make the pattern.* To make the pattern, draw directly on the fabric (folded in half) or on a large sheet of paper, as follows:

- Along the fold, draw a rectangle with the length equal to A and the depth equal to B.

- To plot the chest strap, extend the length of the rectangle about 6" (for small dogs) to 12" (for larger dogs), then divide this section into quarters. These fold-over flaps are designed to adjust to the size of your dog.

- Draw two smooth curves and one half circle in the rectangles as shown. Also draw a curve at the opposite corner (the back of the vest).

- Draw a 3" x 7" rectangle for the belly straps. You will cut four of these to match the double-thickness of the vest body.

3. *Do a test run (optional).* You might want to test the pattern by cutting the body piece from some scrap material before you cut into your fleece fabric. Try the test vest on your dog and check the following items. Make any necessary changes to the pattern.

- Do the length and width fit well?

- Do the chest straps need to be longer or shorter?

- Does the neck curve need to be adjusted?

- Mark the best location for the belly straps.

4. Cut it out. Fold the camouflage fleece with right sides together and the greatest stretch running horizontally. Mark with a pin where the fold-line is located. To get both vest pieces on the fold, open the fleece up and refold each half to meet at the center line. You now have folds on either side; cut a vest piece on each fold. Also from the camouflage fleece, cut four chest straps. From the solid-color waffle fleece, cut two pockets that are 7" x 6". (For a smaller dog you might want smaller pockets.)

5. Stitch the vest. Pin the vest pieces right sides together. Mark about a 4" gap on both sides where the belly straps will be inserted. Stitch the vest pieces together, leaving openings for the belly straps, then turn the vest right sides out through one of the openings.

6. Stitch the belly straps. Pin two pairs of straps right sides together. For each pair, stitch the long sides and one end, leaving one end open. Turn the straps right sides out and topstitch on the sewn sides. Tuck each strap into a vest opening and pin.

7. Topstitch the vest. Topstitch around the entire outer edge of the vest through all layers.

8. Add Velcro. Stitch Velcro to the vest as shown: one square each on the belly straps and two strips each on the chest straps.

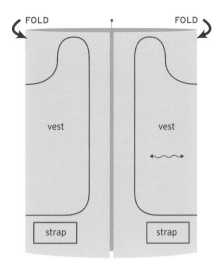

STEP 4

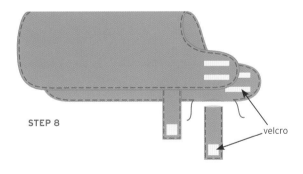

STEP 8

velcro

9. Embellish. Position the twill tape 2" from the center back on both sides, then machine-stitch both sides of the tape through all layers. For the pockets, turn under raw edges by ½" and topstitch in place.

Pooch Pillow

Let sleeping dogs lie in comfort on this cushy dog bed. Any dog will love napping on its soft plush surface. The bone appliqué adds a bit of fun and couldn't be easier to make. Install a zipper to make the cover removable for easy washing. Our pillow is sized for a large dog but make it larger or smaller to suit your dog.

Stuff You Need

1 yard of 58"-60" medium-weight striped fleece

1 yard of 58"-60" heavyweight textured fleece

1½ yards of 45" medium-weight lining fabric (such as pillow ticking or muslin)

1 matching 22" zipper

Polyester fiberfill

Pinking shears

Matching or contrasting polyester thread

What You'll Do

Cut and stitch the inner pillow.

Cut, decorate, and stitch the dog-bed cover.

Our finished size: 30" x 30"

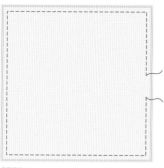

STEP 1

STEP 1

STEP 2

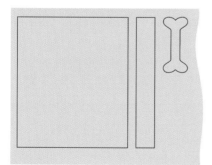

STEP 2

MAKE IT

1. *Make the inner pillow.* From the pillow ticking or muslin, cut two 28" x 28" squares (or the size that best fits your dog). With right sides together, machine-stitch the squares together, leaving a 4" opening for turning. Turn the pillow right sides out and stuff it with polyester fiberfill. Machine-stitch or hand-sew the opening closed.

2. *Cut out the dog bed.* Lay the fabric out smooth on a cutting surface. From the medium-weight fleece, cut out one 30" x 30" square, using pinking shears or any other decorative edge scissors. From the heavyweight fleece, cut one 4½" x 30" rectangle, and a 26½" x 30" rectangle. (These two pieces will be joined with a zipper, so a ½" seam allowance has been added to one side of each piece.)

3. *Cut out the bone.* Practice drawing a dog bone (or any other shape you like) on a piece of paper. When you have the shape you like, cut it from the heavyweight fleece. To draw a bone shape:

- Fold an 8½" x 11" sheet of paper in fourths.

- Draw a shape that looks like a golf club.

- Open the paper and adjust the shape as desired.

pssst...

SHORTCUT

Instead of making the inner pillow for the dog bed, you can purchase a ready-made pillow and make a fleece cover to fit. Or, if your dog already has a favorite pillow, measure it for size and update it with a new fleece cover. Whatever print or colors you choose, we recommend using a medium-weight fleece for the top of the pillow and a heavier-weight fleece for the bottom.

4. *Embellish the cover*. Pin the dog bone to the center of the medium-weight fleece square. Zigzag around the outer edge of the bone.

5. *Install the zipper*. Pin the two heavyweight fabric pieces together along the 30" side.
a. Mark a 22" section where the zipper will go. Machine-stitch the strips together, switching to a long basting stitch for the 22" section.
b. Finger-press the seam open. Pin your zipper face down onto the center of the seam allowance. Machine-stitch the zipper in place and remove the basting stitches. (*See page* 30.)

6. *Stitch the sides*. With wrong sides together, pin the dog bed squares together. Stitch around the squares, 2" from the raw edge, using a zig-zag stitch. Insert the inner pillow into the dog bed cover.

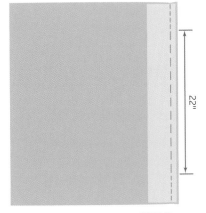

STEP 5a

STEP 5b

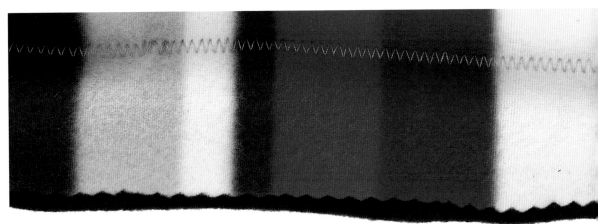

STEP 6

Resources

Periodicals

For sewing ideas, inspiration, and techniques, check out the following magazines:

Clotilde's Sewing Savvy
800-449-0440
www.clotildessewingsavvy.com

Creative Needle
800-443-3127
www.creativeneedlemag.com

Fiberarts
Interweave Press
800-875-6208
www.fiberartsmagazine.com

Sew News
800-289-6397
www.sewnews.com

Threads
The Taunton Press
800-477-8727
www.threadsmagazine.com

Sewing Machine Information

If you're looking for a sewing machine manual or need information or parts for your machine, check out the Web sites below or do a search for the name of your sewing machine manufacturer.

http://sewing.about.com
http://parts.singerco.com
www.sewusa.com
www.tias.com/stores/relics

Fabrics, Notions & Tools

The best way to select fabric is hands-on. Check your local phone book under "fabric shops" or "quilting" for local sources of fleece and other fabrics, tools, and notions.

To order supplies online, the following Web sites are fantastic sources for all your needs and more. Many of these sites provide tips, patterns, and a lot of great ideas.

http://fabrimartfabrics.com
http://sewing.patternreview.com
www.cheeptrims.com
www.denverfabrics.com
www.equilter.com
www.fabricdepot.com
www.fleecelady.com
www.hancockfabrics.com
www.hancocks-paducah.com
www.hymanhendler.com
www.joann.com
www.maldenmillsstore.com
www.millendstore.com
www.mjtrim.com
www.nancysnotions.com
www.patternworks.com
www.questoutfitters.com
www.reprodepotfabrics.com
www.ribbonerie.com
www.seattlefabrics.com
www.snapsource.com
www.stitch-n-frame.net
www.thesewingplace.com
www.tinseltrading.com
www.valleyfabrics.com

Index

Index (continued)

Other Storey Titles You Will Enjoy

Colorful Stitchery, by Kristin Nicolas.
Dozens of embroidered projects to embellish and enhance any home.
208 pages. Paper. ISBN-13: 978-1-58017-611-8.

Felt It!, by Maggie Pace.
Hats, shawls, belts, bags, home accessories — the perfect introduction to
the magic of felting, for all levels of knitters.
152 pages. Paper. ISBN-13: 978-1-58017-635-4.

Knit One, Felt Too, by Kathleen Taylor.
Twenty-five spectacular projects to transform items, knit large and loose,
into thick, cozy, felted garments or accessories.
176 pages. Paper. ISBN-13: 978-1-58017-497-8.

One-Skein Wonders: 101 Yarn Shop Favorites, edited by Judith Durant.
One hundred and one projects for all those single skeins in your stash.
240 pages. Paper. ISBN-13: 978-1-58017-645-3.

Sew What! Skirts, by Francesca DenHartog & Carole Ann Camp.
A fast, straightforward method to sewing a variety of inspired skirts —
without relying on store-bought patterns.
128 pages. Hardcover with concealed wire-o. ISBN-13: 978-1-58017-625-5.

Sewing Packs, Pouches, Seats & Sacks, by Betty Oppenheimer.
More than 30 projects to make practical totes for the home, garden, work-
shop, and camp.
160 pages. Paper. ISBN-13: 978-1-58017-049-9.

These and other books from Storey Publishing are available
wherever quality books are sold or by calling 1-800-441-5700.
Visit us at www.storey.com.